THE MEN WITH THE PINK TRIANGLE

THE MEN WITH THE PINK TRIANGLE

THE TRUE, LIFE-AND-DEATH STORY OF
HOMOSEXUALS IN THE NAZI DEATH CAMPS

HEINZ HEGER

TRANSLATED BY DAVID FERNBACH

Haymarket Books
Chicago, Illinois

Die Männer mit dem rosa Winkel © 1972/2014 MERLIN VER-
LAG Andreas Meyer Verlags GmbH. & Co. KG, Gifkendorf,
Germany

English translation, first published in Great Britain in 1980 by
Gay Men's Press, © 2004 MERLIN VERLAG Andreas Meyer
Verlags GmbH. & Co. KG, Gifkendorf, Germany. Footnotes in
the text are those of the translator.

First published in the United States as a trade paperback original
in 1980 by Alyson Publications Inc. in Los Angeles.
Introduction © 1994 by Dr. Klaus Müller

This edition published in 2023 by
Haymarket Books, P.O. Box 180165, Chicago, IL 60618
www.haymarketbooks.org
info@haymarketbooks.org

ISBN: 978-1-64259-846-9

Distributed to the trade in the US through Consortium Book Sales
and Distribution (www.cbsd.com) and internationally through
Ingram Publisher Services International (www.ingramcontent.com).

This book was published with the generous support of Lannan
Foundation and Wallace Action Fund.

Special discounts are available for bulk purchases by organizations
and institutions. Please call 773-583-7884 or email
info@haymarketbooks.org for more information.

Cover photograph of prisoners in the concentration camp at
Sachsenhausen, Germany, December 12, 1938, courtesy of US
National Archives. Cover design by Matt Avery.

Library of Congress Cataloging-in-Publication data is available.

10 9 8 7 6 5 4 3 2 1

CONTENTS

PUBLISHERS' NOTE

Haymarket Books is honored to bring this poignant and pathbreaking narrative back into print. We are grateful for the collaboration of Merlin Verlag in preparing this edition. Thanks to Sean Larson for translating Heinz Heger's preface and to Caroline Luft for translating the afterword by the estate of Helmut Musatits, each appearing in English for the first time here.

Throughout the book, we have chosen not to alter language the authors or translators selected. These texts therefore retain contested, out-dated, or even prejudicial terms such as "Gypsy," reflecting the historical and political contexts in which they originated.

FOREWORD

THE WORLD WITH THE PINK TRIANGLE

Sarah Schulman

Exterminated homosexuals were never legally acknowledged as victims of the Nazi regime and did not get a Nuremberg. Some even had their incarcerations extended by the "liberating" forces. The Austrian author of this brave and wrenching account, Heinz Heger, conveys the experience described to him by a man put in German concentration camps of Sachsenhausen and Flossenbürg. In contrast to the Jewish yellow star, he was made to wear the pink triangle while lesbians were classified as black triangled "anti-socials" along with Anarchists. The fascists understood the difference in social function of lesbians and gay men in ways that still elude us. The survivor Heger depicts saw himself as "apolitical" even though his family and his lover's family were part of or collaborators with the Nazi regime. He thought his homosexuality was a secret until he was arrested. From the start of his six years of incarceration and physical and emotional trauma, his first lesson was that the pink triangle on his camp uniform meant that he was "out" 24 hours a day, and subject to the special punishments imposed by Nazis. But he also had access to inside corruptions, quickly discovering that straight men typically want and have some kind of gay sex, whether with each other or

with a designated "gay." But he was also able to survive because
he could exchange sexual relationships with Capos, prisoners
who served an intermediary role supervising the slave laborers
for the Nazis. Ultimately this got him protection and food and
eventually a desk job. Here Heger lets us into the social struc-
ture of the camps, how the green triangles (criminals) and red
triangles (politicals) had higher status than Jews, Roma, and
homosexuals. Eventually, when his camp was turned into a
munitions factory, the subject of this account also became a
Capo, and was able to receive bribes of tobacco and money
from other prisoners, until the end of the war.

Hitler and Nazism are a historical reality that also lives in
our contemporary imagination and experience as signals of
and metaphors for cataclysm. There are those of us who are
direct descendants of the victims, the perpetrators, and the
bystanders, the living connections to the events of 1933–1945.
There are those who want to emulate the Nazis, assert Aryan
Supremacy, re-create race laws, separation, and extermination.
Some of us live in opposition to fascists; we see them coming.
We see them in the White House, on television, in the streets,
in the police department. In the current rise of authoritarian
thinking and rule, descendants of German, Polish fascism
are found today on the rise in . . . Poland, Germany, Hungary,
Russia, and also in Arizona, Georgia, Texas, states with forces
intending to suppress voting rights, keep abortion inaccessible,
stop trans people from using bathrooms, keep schools from
teaching about race. The French president warns of so-called
Islamo-fascism in universities, mirroring the anti-Jewish accusation of "Bolshevik bankers." Jewish Israelis demolish Pales-
tinian homes, chanting, "Death to Arabs," and aerial bomb
apartment buildings in Gaza. Preppy White Supremacists in
khakis chant, "The Jews will not replace us," police officers
murder Black civilians regularly and mostly without conse-

quence. The United States is unable to pass a federal anti-discrimination bill protecting queer people's jobs and apartments, while white gay people in nations that grant full equality increasingly join racist anti-immigrant movements. Over and over the paradigms shift. As groups gain access to the powers of nationalism, they take on attributes of supremacy thinking about themselves, and their claims to superiority and desires for dominance resurface again and again.

The systemic and deep oppression of a category of people carries consequences throughout the lives of the victims, and historically through the self-concepts of those who are the inheritors of their legacies. And this consciousness can become a force for expansion of solidarity and demands for justice, or it can be distorted into projections and victimization of new categories of subordinated people. Or it can become an exploited pose, demanding attention and repair for a wound that has never been directly experienced. In queer culture, we don't know who we are if we have full privileges and rights, especially with specific privileges of whiteness and maleness. Often, those who can just become white people, stepping into the nationalisms and advantages our heterosexual and homophobic white ancestors accessed. Or there are Jews who think they are going to the gas chambers tomorrow, while holding state power over an Occupied people. Or Jews living in the diaspora watching anti-Semitism growing. Yet, it remains a prejudice, not taking on a material application as other people are plummeted into refugee status, placed in camps and murdered by their own governments, by uncaring first world neglect of climate change, of murderous regimes, of pointless endless wars. In other words, fascism and authoritarianism depend on victimization and are constantly cycling through nations, diasporas, racial identities, and are expressed in both geopolitical and intimate realms.

The blunt brutality, pain, and corruption of this stark, crucial account provides insight into the untold story of gay men under Nazi fascism, survival in the context of extermination camps, and the peculiar specificity of retaining identity. The man whose story Heger relates was never pure or clean. He was a survivor, and part of his afterlife involves this provocative and insistently accurate telling of how he and other gay men died and lived.

INTRODUCTION

Dr. Klaus Müller[1]

1994

"I'm living proof that Hitler didn't win. I'm aware of that every day." The speaker is Friedrich-Paul von Groszheim. At the age of eighty-eight, this charming gay man celebrates his birthday twice a year. "You never know," he says.

One can hardly imagine the suffering he endured. Von Groszheim was among 230 men arrested in Lübeck in the course of a single evening in 1937. The police hauled him from his home and imprisoned him for ten months. He was released, but re-arrested. This time, the Nazi authorities forced him to choose between castration or incarceration at the concentration camp at Sachsenhausen. He submitted to castration.

His nightmare had not ended, however. In 1943, von Groszheim was arrested a third time, and was put into a satellite camp of Neuengamme. He survived that ordeal, but a full half century would have to pass before he started to tell his story.

---

1   Dr. Klaus Müller is a historian and consultant for the United States Holocaust Memorial Museum in Washington, DC. He acknowledges the work of Richard Plant, author of *The Pink Triangle*, of whose work he considers his own to be a continuation.

PERSECUTION WITHOUT END

Why have so few gay Holocaust survivors come forward to describe their ordeals? Why has it taken so long for their voices to be heard?

In 1945, at the time of liberation, it was common knowledge among the Allied forces that gay men had been prisoners in the Nazi concentration camps, and that they had been marked with a pink triangle. This awareness is documented in the reports of liberators, and in the testimony of survivors. But although they were released from the concentration camps at the close of World War II, homosexuals were not liberated in the fullest sense of the word. Their persecution continued, first under the Allied military government of Germany, later under the German authorities.

Within the realm of Holocaust research, gay men belonged for a long time to the so-called group of forgotten victims—those groups of Holocaust victims who for a long time were not acknowledged as such: the mentally and physically handicapped, prostitutes, alcoholics, the victims of forced sterilization, and all those who were labeled as asocial or otherwise "alienated to the people" under the Nazi regime. Calling homosexual victims of the Nazis "forgotten victims," however, distorts history. The postwar German government did not simply forget about homosexuals; on the contrary, it actively continued to persecute them, and to justify the efforts of the Nazis in this respect.

Gay Holocaust survivors like Friedrich-Paul von Groszheim or Karl Gorath, a survivor of Neuengamme, Auschwitz, and Mauthausen, were never legally acknowledged as victims of the Nazi regime. For them, the fear did not end with the forces of liberation. They lived in continual fear of being re-arrested. Some were treated as repeat offenders after the war, under the same law against homosexuality, Paragraph

175 of the criminal code, that was originally put in place in 1871 and which was revised and strengthened by the Nazis.

The Nazi version of Paragraph 175 was, in fact, explicitly upheld in 1957 by the West German supreme court. Anti-gay laws and prejudice had existed before Hitler came to power, argued the court, and therefore couldn't be seen as peculiar to Nazi ideology.

Of course, anti-Semitism, special laws against Gypsies, and discussions within the medical establishment about sterilization of the disabled had all existed before 1933 as well. Like homophobia, these policies and prejudices took on a new meaning as they were incorporated into Nazi ideology. The supreme court ignored such parallels, however. Further, it ruled, Paragraph 175 was necessary for the protection of the German people.

Not until 1969 would Paragraph 175 be repealed.

THE END OF THE FIRST GAY AND LESBIAN MOVEMENT

There had been a sodomy law on the books since German unification in 1871, but it specifically targeted anal intercourse. Consenting adults rarely filed complaints, and there were few prosecutions under this law. For a brief moment in 1929, the burgeoning gay and lesbian movement even seemed likely to abolish Paragraph 175. A parliamentary commission that was rewriting the nation's moral code voted to drop the anti-sodomy statute. But because of the growing influence of the Nazi party, the commission's recommendation was never introduced in parliament.

After Hitler rose to power, both the Gestapo and the German SS pressed to broaden the old and "inefficient" sodomy law to the extent that it was no longer necessary to provide evidence of having committed outlawed homosexual acts for a suspected homosexual to be arrested and convicted. Homosexuality was not just a criminal offense, argued Nazi leader Heinrich Himmler, but a danger to the future Aryan race. On June 28, 1935, the same year that the Nuremberg laws[2] were enacted, a revised and strengthened Paragraph 175 was enacted. Already the mere suggestion of homosexual intent was grounds for arrest: kissing or embracing another man, gossip spread by neighbors, or receiving a letter from a gay friend were now adequate evidence.

The Nazi persecution of homosexuals came as no surprise. The "Golden Twenties" had seen a flourishing gay and lesbian culture in Germany's urban areas. Gay and lesbian organizations, publishing houses, journals, and social groups and events proliferated; Berlin alone boasted nearly a hundred gay and lesbian bars. Yet even in the midst of this activity, the Nazis made it clear that the future Aryan Reich would have no place for homosexuals.

Soon after taking office in 1933, Hitler banned all gay and lesbian organizations. Storm troopers raided the institutions and gathering places of the gay and lesbian community. The vast and irreplaceable library of the Institute for Sexual Science was destroyed in the famous Berlin book burning of May 1933. The institute, founded by Dr. Magnus Hirschfeld in 1919, had become a world-famous leader in the nascent field of sexology, and Hirschfeld was prominent in Germany's early gay movement. As a gay Jewish man, Hirschfeld was denounced by the Nazi propaganda machine as an early

---

2   The Nuremberg laws drew a distinction between so-called Aryans and non-Aryans. The latter category applied to all non-Germanic peoples, but was applied primarily against Jews, Gypsies, and Afro-Germans. Under the Nuremberg laws, non-Aryans lost their German citizenship and were prohibited from engaging in sexual activity with Germans.

symbol of the "decay" of the Weimar Republic; only the good luck of being on a world tour in 1933 prevented his murder.

Despite the closing of gay bars and the raiding of the Institute for Sexual Science in 1933, some mistook Nazi anti-gay politics as somehow ambivalent so long as SA chief Ernst Röhm was tolerated. Although Röhm was not openly homosexual, his homosexuality was nonetheless widely known. When Hitler suspected Röhm of plotting against him, Röhm and many others were killed on June 30, 1934. Röhm's homosexuality was then cited as a means of justifying the so-called Night of the Long Knives, and Hitler promised in a widely printed public order to rid all Nazi organizations of homosexuals. SS chief Heinrich Himmler carried out this order by creating special police departments and by issuing decrees relating to the racial purity of the SS and police.[3]

Despite Röhm's death in 1934, his homosexuality was used widely in communist propaganda as an example of the "true nature" of the Third Reich. During the 1930s and 1940s, homophobia would become one of the most frequently used tools of both Nazi and Stalinist propaganda to portray the other side as morally degenerate. Postwar films about the Nazi regime often included these homophobic posturings without challenging them. The Nazi anti-gay policies were largely ignored, as were the gay victims of the camps.

After Röhm's murder, Himmler focused his attention on the homosexual "threat." In 1936, the Federal Security Office for combatting abortion and homosexuality was established, further consolidating the connection between National Socialist politics, race improvement, and homophobia.

---

3   On November 15, 1941, for example, Himmler ordered that any
    SS officer or policeman caught "engaging in indecent behavior with
    another man or allowing himself to be abused by him for indecent
    purposes ... be condemned to death and executed."

THE INVISIBLE LESBIAN

It is only partially helpful to compare the experiences of lesbian women with that of gay men in this era. Within the strongly gender-biased society of Nazi Germany, the persecution of gay men became the focus of Nazi anti-gay politics. Nazi ideology defined male homosexuals as enemies of the state, and from 1934 onward, gay men were persecuted relentlessly. Only gay men were made criminals under Paragraph 175; we know much less about the persecution of lesbians under this regime than we do about the fate of gay men during the same period.

Of course, lesbians, like their male counterparts, were forced to go underground. According to the few testimonies that have reached us, many lesbians got married, often to gay friends, to protect themselves and their gay friends. Throughout the thirties and early forties, Nazi officials debated the merits of including lesbianism in Paragraph 175. Ultimately, three arguments prevented that step. First, lesbianism was seen by many Nazi officials as essentially alien to the nature of the "Aryan" woman. Second, since women were largely excluded from positions of power, there seemed to be no real danger of a "lesbian conspiracy" within high Nazi circles. (There *were* concerns that homosexual men might embark on such a conspiracy.) The third and most cynical argument was also the most influential: "Aryan" lesbians could be used as breeders regardless of their own feelings, and reproduction was the most urgent goal of Nazi population politics.

We know only a few documented cases of lesbians being incarcerated in the concentration camps solely because of their sexual orientation. We have no historical evidence that lesbians were systematically marked with pink triangles or black triangles. Those few accounts we do have disagree on this point. We have glimpses of lesbian relationships in the camps through the autobiographical accounts of Jewish and political prisoners who survived, but these accounts are sketchy.

The lives of lesbians were shaped less by official Nazi homophobia than by the regime's marginalization of women in general, and its contempt for female sexuality. State propaganda exalted marriage and motherhood; the ideal German woman was the breeder of a future "Aryan" race. A woman who was openly lesbian had no place in this scenario, of course, but we know few details about the difficult position of lesbians in Nazi Germany.

THE PINK TRIANGLE

Police raids and mass arrests of homosexual men became common at the end of 1934, when many homosexuals were sent to the first established concentration camps. Their uniforms sometimes bore an identifying mark such as the letter *A* (from the German word for "ass-fucker"). This mark was later replaced by a pink triangle.

Not until the late 1980s and early 1990s did researchers begin seriously to explore the Nazi persecution of homosexuals, and many important questions remain unanswered. An early study estimated that ten to fifteen thousand men had worn the pink triangle. This figure is widely quoted and remains the best available estimate, but there has never been a systematic survey of the number of male homosexuals in different camps. Such a survey is greatly overdue.

Nor do we know why certain camps (such as the smaller Emsland camps) had a relatively higher percentage of gay prisoners. Finally, we know that homosexuals were sometimes placed into special slave-labor squads, and were subjected to medical experiments, but little further research has been done in these areas. At Buchenwald, for example, an SS doctor performed operations designed to transform gay men into heterosexuals through the surgical insertion of a capsule which released the male hormone, testosterone; some of the men died during the operation. Such procedures reflected the desire by Himmler and others to find a medical "solution" to homosexuality.

A pink triangle meant harsher treatment in the camps. Gay men suffered a higher mortality rate than did other relatively small victim groups, such as Jehovah's Witnesses and political prisoners. The men with the pink triangle couldn't count on a support network within the camps, and were often treated with contempt by their fellow prisoners. Many were given the hardest work, and died within a few months of arrival. Sometimes gay men were segregated in special 175 barracks. There is little documentation on the treatment of Jewish camp inmates who were also marked with a pink triangle. However, some testimonies suggest a pattern of special brutality during police raids toward gay men who were discovered to be Jewish as well.

Although the pink triangle has become an international emblem of the gay and lesbian community today, we still know little about the individual fate of those who suffered wearing it. A symbol invented by the Nazis, the pink triangle was able to become a modern symbol of gay and lesbian pride only because we are not haunted by concrete memories of those who were forced to wear it in the camps. Ours is an empty memory. We have few names, and fewer faces: not more than fifteen gay Holocaust survivors have spoken of their experiences, and many of them have asked for anonymity.

This is understandable, given the world into which they were released in 1945. Unlike other survivors, the gay prisoners soon discovered that their persecution had not ended. Their concentration camp imprisonment became a part of their police record, and increased their vulnerability to police raids. Throughout the 1950s and 1960s, German courts convicted homosexual men at a rate as high as that of the Nazi regime. Having survived the concentration camps, some men could not find the strength to face this second wave of persecution. We know of several cases where, after the war, concentration camp survivors were charged for violations of Paragraph 175 and committed suicide either before the trial or afterward in prison. Still more escaped into marriage or into complete isolation.

While other Holocaust survivors were recognized as survivors by the outside world, the men who wore the pink triangle never received that recognition. They were ignored in the memorials and in the museums. Still seen as criminals and perverts, they never had an opportunity to regain their dignity in postwar society. They survived, but they were denied their place in the community of survivors.

That exclusion from the memory of the Holocaust took a toll on individual memories. Most gay survivors are reluctant to be interviewed. As they tell their story they stop themselves, expressing doubts that "anyone is interested to hear that anyway."

Gay Holocaust survivors received no moral or financial support after 1945—not from the government, not from Holocaust researchers, not from the fragile gay and lesbian community. As a result, some internalized Nazi persecution as their own fault, blaming themselves for not having been smarter in hiding their lives. "It all happened because we stupid queens didn't hide our address books," one survivor told me. Others, showing astonishing courage for their time, tried to be recognized after the war as victims of the Nazi regime, but they lost their battles in court.

Karl Gorath was one who fought for that recognition. Gorath was twenty-six in 1939 when his jealous lover denounced him to the Gestapo. As an SS guard held a gun to his head, Gorath was forced to sign a confession. He never saw a court or a judge, and was brought to the concentration camp of Neuengamme, then to Wittenberge (Elbe) in 1940.

When he refused to reduce the bread rations for Soviet prisoners of war, Gorath was sent on a penal transport to Auschwitz in 1942. He managed to switch his pink triangle for a red one en route, an act that probably saved his life. Shortly before Auschwitz was liberated, he and other inmates were sent to the camp at Mauthausen, and later to camps at Melk and Ebensee. After finally being liberated by the US Army in 1945, he nearly died of cholera.

In 1949, Gorath was sentenced to four years in prison for violation of Paragraph 175. He asked for reparations from the German government in 1953 and again in 1960. Both times his request was refused: in the eyes of the German government, homosexuals were not victims of the Nazi regime. Today, 81-year-old Karl Gorath lives in Germany, and has never received the financial compensation given to other Holocaust survivors.

THE UNITED STATES HOLOCAUST MEMORIAL MUSEUM

The German government may have forgotten Karl Gorath, but elsewhere he has, at last, been acknowledged as a survivor. Gorath's story is one of nine that are documented in the unique ID card project of the United States Holocaust Memorial Museum, an act of inclusion that amazes him. Documenting individual gay victims of the Holocaust turned out be a very difficult undertaking. Of the testimony that does exist, much was given anonymously—at first, survivors were hesitant to provide their full names—while others described only a portion of an individual's experiences and suffering. This museum is the first major Holocaust institution to conscientiously integrate the experience of homosexuals into its exhibits and educational programs. It is a step long overdue: according to a recent survey commissioned by the American Jewish Committee, only about half of the adults in Britain, and a mere quarter of adults in the United States, know that gays were victims of the Nazi Holocaust.

Archives throughout the US contain several thousand testimonies given by survivors of the Holocaust, but none are from gay or lesbian survivors: the questionnaires guiding these interviews did not include questions about the fate of those marked with the pink triangle. There is an abundance of excellent Holocaust research literature, but only one book available in English provides a first-person account of the men with the pink triangle. Homophobia has never been discussed within Holocaust studies as an important part of Nazi propaganda, racism, and population politics.

It has taken five decades for a museum or memorial to officially recognize the truth. It will take longer still to counteract the damage inflicted by fifty years of official, scholarly, and social neglect. *The Men with the Pink Triangle* offers a glimpse of a seldom-discussed and barely explored history, a memory almost forgotten. At last, we are ensuring that this memory will survive.

Hundreds of thousands of non-Jews were sent by the Nazis to concentration camps. They included Socialists, Gypsies, the mentally ill, Jehovah's Witnesses, and homosexuals.

North Sea

Baltic Sea

Vaivara

Klooga
ESTONIA

LATVIA

LITHUANIA

USSR

Stutthof

Neuengamme   Ravensbrück

Treblinka

Bergen-Belsen   Sachsenhausen   Chelmno

Mittelbau Dora   Gross Rosen   POLAND   Sobibor

Buchenwald   Maidanek

GERMANY   Auschwitz

Flossenbürg   Plaszow   Belzec

Natzweiler   CZECHOSLOVAKIA

FRANCE   Dachau

Mauthausen

AUSTRIA   HUNGARY   RUMANIA

Gospič   Jasenovač

Sajmište

ITALY

Adriatic Sea

YUGOSLAVIA

Concentration camp in which more than four million people were murdered by the Nazis from 1941 to 1945.

Camps set up solely for the murder of Jews.

Other camps, in which Jews and non-Jews were put to forced labor, starved, tortured, and killed.

PREFACE

Heinz Heger

AFTER THE "RÖHM PUTSCH" in 1934, the National Socialist German state increased the legal restrictions on homosexuality. Paragraph 175a was added to the relevant criminal laws, which significantly increased the already-existing penalties.

Tens of thousands, probably hundreds of thousands of homosexuals were thrown into the concentration camps during the National Socialist regime up to 1945 and had to wear their pink triangles there. All of them were mercilessly delivered to the whims of the SS henchmen, suffering torture and torment until death set them free. To this day, it is not known exactly how many men wearing the pink triangle were imprisoned in the various Nazi concentration camps, because no accurate records were kept for this category of prisoners. According to the well-known hypothesis by Kinsey, that around 4 to 5 percent of the population perceive are homosexual, there were around two million homosexuals in Germany at the time. One can therefore assume with a certain plausibility that there were several hundred thousand concentration camp prisoners with the pink triangle.

Not all who wore this triangle were homosexuals. A denunciation was enough to plunge the disfavored into ruin, for example in the case of the unmarried or childless. Even the assumption that one could be a "175er" could be enough to be taken into custody. And those who ended up in the devil's mill of the concentration camp with a pink triangle rarely escaped with their lives. It remains unknown how many men with the pink triangle survived their ordeal. Partly out of shame and partly out of fear, the few victims who were left kept quiet about their concentration camp imprisonment, because in Germany as in Austria homosexuality was and still is considered a crime in some cases; they would therefore have been turned over to renewed harassment by the new democratic authorities. They were threatened with registration as homosexuals, with fingerprints and mug shots in the police books, professional discrimination, social ostracism and ultimately imprisonment again. Since those with pink triangles in the concentration camps were considered criminal inmates, these prisoners were excluded from all reparations, and it was therefore better for their safety if they kept their concentration camp imprisonment a secret.

We do not yet know the exact reasons for homosexuality as a phenomenon, but we already know scientifically that it is not a disease, but a act of nature, a variant of human sensitivity, which affects one in every twelve men and one in every twelve women. According to Kinsey, each population, in America as in Europe, has four percent pure homosexuals and about four percent bisexuals.

Sexual activity among homosexuals differs in no fundamental way from that between heterosexuals. Among homosexuals, we find every kind of sexuality that we find in heterosexuals, from the romantic platonic infatuation for a partner to the perverse orgy. Homosexuals are not misogynists or women-haters, their sex drive is simply directed toward their own sex. As long as children or adolescents are not abused, homosexuality harms neither the person nor the population or state—just as little as the practice of heterosexuality. In today's age of humanity and tolerance, our sex lives should remain an intimate sphere for each individual, in which neither the state nor "good neighbors" are allowed to interfere. One might as well condemn and then criminalize a person's left-handedness or color blindness.

This writer did not himself have to endure the treatment described in this book, rather he wants only to reproduce what was told and shown to him by one of the very few surviving men with the pink triangle. The almost unbelievable harassment and torture, the atrocities should still shame us today for having been followers and fellow human beings of those SS devils. But we should also be ashamed that we have not yet done anything for this category of victims of that "German master race." Curiously, very little is currently known about the suffering of the men with the pink triangle. Many books have written about the assuredly grave fate of the Jews, the "politicals" and the Gypsies, but the men with the pink triangle have only been mentioned in passing, if at all. And yet, just like the Jews, they had to experience and endure all the sadistic violence of the Nazi regime, and they were doomed to die already upon their arrival at the concentration camp.

For the sake of humanity and to help prevent such barbarism from ever being repeated among our people, the author has tried to write down all the sufferings, experiences and feelings of his confidant. Nothing was concealed, nothing exaggerated, and nothing embellished. In its frank and unvarnished language, may this book be regarded as a harsh indictment of the authorities of the Third Reich at the time and of the bestial methods of the Gestapo and the SS, which ruled the entire police apparatus in National Socialist Germany.

It should also give food for thought to those who still believe that it is possible in the long term to live together as a people without openness and tolerance, in a state or on a continent, and who still cannot rid themselves of their beliefs in authoritarian governance.

Let those who are free from all guilt cast the first stone . . .

1

IMPRISONED AS A "DEGENERATE"

VIENNA, MARCH 1939. I was twenty-two years old, a university student preparing for an academic career, a choice that met my parents' wishes as much as my own. Being little interested in politics, I was not a member of the Nazi student association or any of the party's other organizations.

It wasn't as if I had anything special against the new Germany. German was and still is my mother tongue, after all. Yet my upbringing had always been more Austrian in character. I had learned a certain tolerance from my parents, and at home we made no distinction between people for speaking a different language from ours, practicing a different religion, or having a different color of skin. We also respected other people's opinions, no matter how strange they might seem.

I found it far too arrogant, then, when so much started to be said at university about the German master race, our nation chosen by destiny to lead and rule all Europe. For this reason alone, I was already not particularly keen on the new Nazi masters of Austria and their ideas.

My family was well-to-do and strictly Catholic. My father was a senior civil servant, pedantic and correct in all his actions, and always a respected model for me and my three younger sisters. He would admonish us calmly and sensibly if we made too much of a row, and he always spoke of my mother as the lady of the house. He had a deep respect for her, and as far as I can recall, he never let her birthday or saint's day pass without bringing her flowers.

My mother, who is still alive today, has always been the very embodiment of kindness and care for us children, ever ready to help when one of us was in trouble. She could certainly scold if need be, but she was never angry with us for long, and never resentful. She was not only mother to us, but always a good friend as well, whom we could trust with all our secrets and who always had an answer even in the most desperate situation.

Ever since I was sixteen I knew that I was more attracted to my own sex than I was to girls. At first I didn't think this was anything special, but when my school friends began to get romantically involved with girls, while I was still stuck on another boy, I had to give some thought to what this meant.

I was always happy enough in the company of girls, and enjoyed being around them. But I came to realize early on that I valued them more as fellow students, with the same problems and concerns at school, rather than lusting after them like the other boys. The fact that I was homosexual never led me to feel the slightest repulsion for women or girls—quite the opposite. It was simply that I couldn't get involved in a love affair with them; that was foreign to my very nature, even though I tried it a few times.

For three years I managed to keep my homoerotic feelings secret even from my mother, though I found it hard not to be able to speak about this to anyone. In the end, however, I confided in her and told her everything that was necessary to get it off my chest—not so much to ask her advice, however, as simply to end this burden of secrecy.

"My dear child," she replied, "it's your life, and you must live it. No one can slip out of one skin and into another; you have to make the best of what you are. If you think you can find happiness only with another man, that doesn't make you in any way inferior. Just be careful to avoid bad company, and guard against blackmail, as this is a possible danger. Try to find a lasting friendship, as this will protect you from many perils. I've suspected it for a long time, anyway. You have no need at all to despair. Follow my advice, and remember, whatever happens, you are my son and can always come to me with your problems."

I was very much heartened by my mother's reasonable words. Not that I really expected anything else, as she always remained her children's best friend.

At university I got to know several students with views, or, rather, feelings, similar to my own. We formed an informal group, small at first, though after the German invasion and the *"Anschluss"* this was soon enlarged by students from the Reich. Naturally enough, we didn't just help one another with our work. Couples soon formed too, and at the end of 1938 I met the great love of my life.

Fred was the son of a high Nazi official from the Reich, two years older than I, and set on completing his study of medicine at the world-famous Vienna medical school. He was forceful, but at the same time sensitive, and his masculine appearance, success in sport, and great knowledge made such an impression on me that I fell for him straightaway. I must have pleased him too, I suppose, with my Viennese charm and temperament. I also had an athletic figure, which he liked. We were very happy together, and made all kinds of plans for the future, believing we would nevermore be separated.

It was on a Friday, about 1 p.m., almost a year to the day since Austria had become simply the "Ostmark," that I heard two rings at the door. Short, but somehow commanding.

When I opened I was surprised to see a man with a slouch hat and leather coat. With the curt word "Gestapo," he handed me a card with the printed summons to appear for questioning at 2 p.m. at the Gestapo headquarters in the Hotel Metropol.

My mother and I were very upset, but I could only think it had to do with something at the university, possibly a political investigation into a student who had fallen foul of the Nazi student association.

"It can't be anything serious," I told my mother, "otherwise the Gestapo would have taken me off right away."

My mother was still not satisfied, and showed great concern. I, too, had a nervous feeling in my stomach, but then doesn't anyone in a time of dictatorship if they are called in by the secret police?

I happened to glance out of the window and saw the Gestapo man a few doors farther along, standing in front of a shop. It seemed he still had his eye on our door, rather than on the items on display.

Presumably his job was to prevent any attempt by me to escape. He was undoubtedly going to follow me to the hotel. This was extremely unpleasant to contemplate, and I could already feel the threatening danger.

My mother must have felt the same, for when I said goodbye to her she embraced me very warmly and repeated: "Be careful, child, be careful!"

Neither of us thought, however, that we would not meet again for six years, myself a human wreck, she a broken woman, tormented as to the fate of her son, and having had to face the contempt of neighbors and fellow citizens ever since it was known her son was homosexual and had been sent to a concentration camp.

I never saw my father again. It was only after my liberation in 1945 that I learned from my mother how he had tried time and again to secure my release, applying to the interior ministry, the Vienna *Gauleitung,* and the Central Security Department in Berlin. Despite his many connections as a high civil servant, he was continually refused.

Because of these requests, but above all because his son was imprisoned for homosexuality, and this was incompatible with his official position under the Nazi regime, he was forced to retire on reduced pension in December 1940. He could no longer put up with the abuse he received, and in 1942 took his own life—filled with bitterness and grief for an age he could not fit into, filled with disappointment over all those friends who either couldn't or wouldn't help him. He wrote a farewell letter to my mother, asking her forgiveness for having to leave her alone. My mother still has the letter today, and the last lines read: "and so I can no longer tolerate the scorn of my acquaintances and colleagues, and of our neighbors. It's just too much for me! Please forgive me again. God protect our son!"

At five to two I reached the Gestapo HQ. It was a hive of activity, SS men coming and going, men in Nazi uniforms or with the gold party badge hurrying through the corridors and up the stairs. Some men in civilian clothes passed me just as I came through the front door. You could see from their faces that they were very glad to have gotten out of the building.

I showed my summons, and an SS man took me to department IIs. We stopped outside a room with a large sign indicating the official within, until a secretary sitting in the antechamber, also in SS uniform, showed us in. "Your appointment, *Herr Doktor!*" The SS man handed in my card, clicked his heels, and vanished.

The "doctor," in civilian clothes, but with the short, angular haircut and smooth-shaven face that immediately gave him away as a senior officer, sat behind an imposing desk piled up with files, all neatly arranged. He neither greeted me nor even looked at me, but just carried on writing.

I stood and waited. Still nothing happened, for several minutes. The room was quite silent and I scarcely dared breathe, while he steadily wrote on. The only sound was the scratch of his pen. I became more and more nervous, though I recognized the "softening-up" tactic. Quite suddenly he laid down his pen and stared at me with cold gray eyes: "You are a queer, a homosexual, do you admit it?"

"No, no, it's not true," I stammered, almost stunned by his accusation, which was the last thing I expected. I had only thought of some political affair, perhaps to do with the university; now I suddenly found my well-kept secret was out.

"Don't you lie, you dirty queer!" he shouted angrily. "I have clear proof, look at this."

He took a postcard-sized photo from his drawer. "Do you know him?"

His long hairy finger pointed at the picture. Of course I knew the photo. It was a snap someone had taken showing Fred and me with our arms in friendly fashion around each other's shoulders.

"Yes, that's my student friend Fred X."

"Indeed," he said calmly, yet unexpectedly quick: "You've done filthy things together, don't you admit?" His voice was contemptuous, cold, and cutting.

I just shook my head. I couldn't get a word out; it was as if a cord were tied round my neck. A whole world came tumbling down inside me, the world of friendship and love for Fred. Our plans for the future, to stay faithful together, and never to reveal our friendship to outsiders, all this seemed betrayed. I was trembling with agitation, not only because of the "doctor's" examination, but also because our friendship was now revealed. The "doctor" took the picture and turned it over. On it read:

"To my friend Fred in eternal love and deepest affection!" I knew as soon as he showed me the photo that it had my vow of love on the other side. I had given it to Fred for Christmas 1938. It must have got into the wrong hands, I immediately thought. Perhaps his father had found it, though that seemed quite improbable, as he didn't bother much about his son, or at least that was how it seemed. But now the photo was here on the table, before me and the Gestapo man.

"Is that your writing and your signature?" I nodded, tears rising to my eyes.

"That's all, then," he said jovially, content. "Sign here."

He handed me a sheet half written on, which I signed with trembling hand. The letters swam in front of my eyes, my tears now flowing openly. The SS man who had brought me here was now back in the room again.

"Take him away," said the "doctor," giving the SS man a slip of paper and bending over his files again, not deeming me worthy of further attention.

I was taken the same day to the police prison on Rossauer-lände street, which we Viennese know as the "Liesl," as the street used to be called the Elisabethpromenade.

My pressing request to telephone my mother to tell her where I'd been taken was met with the words: "She'll soon know you're not coming home again."

I was then examined bodily, which was very distressing, as I had to undress completely so that the policeman could make sure I was not hiding any forbidden object, even having to bend over. Then I could get dressed again, though my belt and shoelaces were taken away. I was locked in a cell designed for one person, though it already had two other occupants. My fellow prisoners were criminals, one under investigation for housebreaking, the other for swindling widows on the lookout for a new husband. They immediately wanted to know what I was in for, which I refused to tell them. I simply said that I didn't know myself. From what they told me, they were both married, and between thirty and thirty-five years old.

When they found out that I was "queer," as one of the policemen gleefully told them, they immediately made open advances to me, which I angrily rejected. First, I was in no mood for amorous adventures, and in any case, as I told them in no uncertain terms, I wasn't the kind of person who gave himself to anyone.

They then started to insult me and "the whole brood of queers," who ought to be exterminated. It was an unheard-of insult that the authorities should have put a subhuman such as this in the same cell as two relatively decent people. Even if they had come into conflict with the law, they were at least normal men and not moral degenerates. They were on a quite different level from homos, who should be classed as animals. They went on with such insults for quite a while, stressing all the time how they were decent men in comparison with the filthy queers. You'd have thought from their language that it was me who had propositioned them, not the other way round.

As it happened, I found out the very first night that they had sex together, not even caring whether I saw or heard. But in their view—the view of "normal" people—this was only an emergency outlet, with nothing queer about it.

As if you could divide homosexuality into normal and abnormal. I later had the misfortune to discover that it wasn't only these two gangsters who had that opinion, but almost all "normal" men. I still wonder today how this division between normal and abnormal is made. Is there a normal hunger and an abnormal one? A normal thirst and an abnormal one? Isn't hunger always hunger, and thirst thirst? What a hypocritical and illogical way of thinking!

Two weeks later, my trial was already up, justice showing an unusual haste in my case. Under Paragraph 175 of the German criminal code, I was condemned by an Austrian court for homosexual behavior, and sentenced to six months' penal servitude with the added provision of one fast day a month.

Proceedings against the second accused, my friend Fred, were dropped on the grounds of "mental confusion." No exact explanation was given as to what this involved, and it was clear enough from the judge's face that he was less than happy with this formula. Never mind, in Hitler's Third Reich even the judges, supposedly so independent, had to adapt to Nazi reasons of state.

Some "higher power" had put in a finger and influenced the court proceedings. Presumably Fred's father had used his weight as a Nazi high-up, and managed to get his son out of trouble.

For my part, however, I was later to find that the same "power" continued its persecution after my sentence was up. I was not to be released again, so that no one would know that the son of a high Nazi party and state leader was homosexual and mixed up in a criminal trial. It then became clear to me why the Gestapo had involved itself in a harmless "queer case."[1]

I never found out whether Fred had been interrogated by the Gestapo, nor did I see him in court. He was referred to throughout simply as the second accused, and never mentioned by name. He vanished from my sight, and remains so today. After 1945, I tried to find out what had become of him and whether he was still alive, but in vain. His father is said to have shot himself at the end of the war.

---

1   This is of course true, but dispatch to concentration camp, or *Schutzhaft* (= protective custody) in the Nazi euphemism, was by this time automatic after a prison sentence for homosexuality.

I was transferred to the Vienna district prison to serve my sentence. Once again the same bodily examination as in the police station, then I was put in a single cell. Only two days later, however, I was assigned for domestic work on my floor, as a *"faci"* in the prison slang. Three times a day I had to serve meals, going from cell to cell, accompanied of course by a warder, and once a week I had to collect all the prisoners' shirts and give out clean ones. Every day I had to wash the corridors morning and afternoon, and do whatever other services might be needed by the warders (happily though not sexual services!).

This work made my time in prison very much easier. And on top of this, we *facis* were only locked in at 6 p.m. and our cells opened again at 5 a.m., even if we were only permitted to leave them when we had work to do.

In this way I came into contact with many prisoners, and often helped smuggle messages from one cell to another. Several times I had to serve someone condemned to death their last meal, generally a wiener schnitzel and potato salad, knowing that at 4 a.m. the next morning they would be hanged or beheaded. Some of them were political prisoners, resistance fighters against the Nazi regime. I later learned in concentration camp that the Nazis had subsequently abolished even this little humanitarian gesture.

Through these contacts with political detainees, Jews, criminals, and others like myself I discovered a great deal about the misery and suffering inflicted by the Nazis. Up till then I had known very little of the martyrdom of these victims, and this made me stronger and more mature, helping me to bear my long years in concentration camp.

In the Vienna prison, however, we were treated with perfect correctness. Even though the warders were strict in enforcing regulations, they often had a friendly word for us prisoners. Not once during my six months there did I hear of a prisoner being beaten.

On the day that my six months were up, and I should have been released, I was informed that the Central Security Department had demanded that I remain in custody. I was again transferred to the "Liesl," for transit to a concentration camp.

This news was like a blow on the head, for I knew from other prisoners who had been sent back from concentration camp for trial that we "queers," just like the Jews, were tortured to death in the camps, and only rarely came out alive. At that time, however, I couldn't, or wouldn't, believe this. I thought it was exaggeration, designed to upset me. Unfortunately, it was only too true!

And what had I done to be sent off in this way? What infamous crime or damage to the community? I had loved a friend of mine, a grown man of twenty-four, not a child. I could find nothing dreadful or wrong in that.

What does it say about the world we live in, if an adult man is told how and whom he should love? Isn't it always those lawmakers who are sexually inhibited and have inferiority complexes who raise the loudest hue and cry about the alleged "healthy feelings" of their fellow citizens?

2

ARRIVAL AT SACHSENHAUSEN

BY JANUARY 1940 the complement for the transport was made up, and we were to be taken to a camp. One night we were loaded thirty to forty at a time into "green Henrys," the police wagons, and driven to a freight station where a prison train was already waiting. This train consisted mainly of cattle trucks with heavily barred open windows, as well as so-called cell wagons. These were also cattle trucks, but divided up into five or six cells, similarly barred, and set aside for the worst criminals.

I was placed in one of these cells, together with two young men of about my age. We remained together the whole journey. This lasted thirteen days, and proceeded via Salzburg, Munich, Frankfurt, and Leipzig to Berlin-Oranienburg. Each evening we were put off the train and taken to a prison to spend the night, sometimes by truck, but other times on foot. If we went on foot, we had to march in long, heavy chains. These gave a ghostly rattle, like a slave caravan in the depths of the Middle Ages, and passersby would stare fixedly at us in terror.

The cells in the cell wagons only had proper room for one person, with a wooden table and bench. That was the entire furniture, not even a water jug or chamber pot. We were fed only in the evening, at the prisons where we stopped overnight, also being given there a large piece of bread to take on the train the next day. If the train was to stay clean, then we could only attend to the wants of nature at night.

I discovered the very first day that my two young companions were robbers, condemned to death for a murder. What they were doing in the concentration-camp transport was clear neither to them nor to me. They were quite unperturbed, and with a certain grisly pride they took turns in describing the details of their crime. I felt more than uncomfortable in their company, but could hardly do anything about it.

They soon got it out of me that I was a "175er," a "filthy queer," as they called me from then on. They, too, spoke of homosexuals with utter contempt; it didn't bother them that as murderers, they were certainly even more rejected by society. They emphasized, however, that they were at least "normal men."

Normal they may well have been, but the day was long and the guards traveled only in the first and last carriages, so that we had no direct supervision during the journey. So they both said they were getting bored, and wanted a bit of fun. With thumps and blows they forced me to suck their cocks, which I never would have done voluntarily, and this went on several times a day from then on. As far as they were concerned I was a "filthy queer" and must have got the same satisfaction as they did.

For me, however, the whole business was repulsive and made me sick, yet wretched as I felt I was completely in their power. They had no conception that sex had anything to do with emotional feelings and the desire for human contact— even among homosexuals. All that they cared about was a little bit of pleasure for themselves. The whole time, moreover, they spoke obscenely and contemptuously of me and other "filthy queers." *They* weren't queer at all, but quite normal, no matter that it was they who had forced their cocks into my mouth. A strange "normality"!

When we reached the Oranienburg station, we were again loaded up a ramp onto trucks and driven to Sachsenhausen camp.

To make my experience in concentration camp a bit more comprehensible, I should first of all describe how the camps were constructed and run.

Almost every concentration camp had three different zones. The prison camp itself was made up of a large number of wooden barracks, or "blocks," where the prisoners lived. These were divided by wide roads, then there were buildings for the kitchen, laundry, sick bay, and other facilities, including a mortuary and crematorium. Most important was the big parade ground, where the worst excesses of the SS butchers were generally carried out, and behind it the camp gate with buildings on either side. One of these buildings, known as the "bunker," contained the arrest cells, the other the offices of the prison-camp commanders and the guard room. The whole prisoners' zone was surrounded by a barbed-wire fence more than three meters high, which in several camps was electrified. Outside the barbed wire stood several watchtowers at regular intervals, always occupied by SS guards. The gate had its own tower, with a platform from which the entire prisoners' zone could be surveyed, and if need be fired upon by the machine guns placed there.

The garrison zone, which lay outside the barbed-wire surround of the prisoners' zone, contained the headquarters building, the various administrative buildings and offices, the barracks of the SS guard battalion, the homes of the senior SS officers, the officers' and NCOs' clubs, and usually a riding stable, as well as other facilities such as a vegetable garden, poultry farm, and so on.

The third zone was the SS residential area, well away from the other zones, and in a more pleasant setting. It contained nice family homes where the SS officers and NCOs lived with their families, when they did not have quarters in the garrison zone.

Each of our blocks had two wings, wing A on the left, wing B on the right. In the middle were the washroom and lavatories. Each wing contained a dormitory and a dayroom. The dormitory had bunks in three tiers, accommodating from 150 to 300 prisoners. What little free time we had could only be spent in the dayroom, it being strictly forbidden to enter the dormitory during the daytime. The dayroom was equipped with tables and benches, and each prisoner had to keep his few belongings and eating utensils in a wooden cabinet divided into drawers.

Each concentration camp had a camp SS, responsible for the internal management of the prison camp, and an SS guard battalion, who stood guard outside the wire, occupied the main watchtower, and patrolled the camp perimeter.

At the head of the entire camp stood the commandant, with his adjutants and the senior administrative officer. Next came the commanders of the camp SS, generally two in number, who had direct charge of the prison camp and were immediately under the commandant. These were the real and immediate masters of the concentration camp, and exercised an unmitigated violence in the prisoners' zone. Below them stood the report officers, again usually two, who had to report on the prisoners' records and files. Under them in turn were the SS block leaders. These had complete power over the prisoners in their block, and although they had to account to the report officers for everything that went on there, no constraints were ever placed on their brutal and murderous conduct against the prisoners. Indeed, orders and instructions from headquarters constantly incited them to treat the inmates still more severely. These block leaders committed the great majority of atrocities and killings. At the same level as the block leaders there stood the SS work detachment leaders. Block leaders and work detachment leaders were all NCOs, while report officers and camp commanders were commissioned officers, from *SS Untersturmführer* upward.

Subaltern functions in the camp administration were performed by selected prisoners, and the SS also appointed a camp senior. He stood over the other prisoners and was responsible for them to the SS camp commanders. This was an extremely dangerous position, requiring a good deal of courage and imagination, but often being for all that a passive tool in the hands of the SS. It was a difficult job, for too many interventions on behalf of the prisoners cost many of these seniors their necks.

The prisoners' office, of which the camp senior was in charge, came under the authority of the report officers, and was exclusively staffed by prisoners. This regulated the immediate internal management of the prison camp, including such things as the composition of work detachments, the distribution of rations, preparation for parades, and so on.

Each block similarly had a block senior, responsible for the block from the prisoners' side. These had to account to the SS block leaders for everything that happened or was supposed to happen within the block, and they were powerful lords over their fellow prisoners. Together with the camp senior and the *Obercapos*, they made up the camp "dignitaries." They, too, had power of life and death over those in their charge. In the concentration camps every prisoner always had two masters to crack the whip over him: the butchers of the SS and the "dignitaries" from his own ranks.

For each of the two wings in a block, the block seniors appointed one or two orderlies, in charge of keeping their wing or room clean and tidy, and for distributing food. The Capos were again prisoners, in charge of the work detachments and responsible to the SS work leader for the appointed quota of work having been performed. Under them they had foremen. Sometimes several work detachments in one division—for example, building division, quarrying division, and so on—were put in the charge of a senior SS detachment leader and an *Obercapo*.

All the positions of "dignitaries," from the camp senior down to the lowest Capo, were filled—with very few exceptions—only by prisoners with red or green triangles—that is, politicals or criminals. They greatly abused the very real power that they had, especially the greens. Corruption and tyranny toward their fellow prisoners was especially rife in their ranks, and where brutality was concerned they were in no way behind the SS, particularly in dealing with those of us with the pink triangle.

As their badge of office they wore a black armband with the initials of their position in white, for example, LA for camp senior *(Lagerälteste)*, BA for block senior *(Blockälteste)*.

The prisoners' uniforms were marked with a colored cloth triangle to denote their offense or origin. Their prison number was sewn below the triangle. The triangle was about five centimeters across and placed point down, and was stitched onto the left breast of the jacket and coat and the outside right trouser leg.

The colors of the triangles were as follows:

yellow for Jews,	black for anti-socials,
red for politicals,	purple for Jehovah's Witnesses,
green for criminals,	blue for emigrants,
pink for homosexuals,	brown for Gypsies.

The pink triangle, however, was about 2 or 3 centimeters larger than the others, so that we could be clearly recognized from a distance.

Jews, homosexuals, and Gypsies, the yellow, pink, and brown triangles, were the prisoners who suffered most frequently and most severely from the tortures and blows of the SS and the Capos. They were described as the scum of humanity, who had no right to live on German soil and should be exterminated. Such were the oft-repeated words of the commandant and his SS subordinates. But the lowest of the low in this "scum" were we, the men with the pink triangle.

As soon as we were unloaded on the large, open parade ground, some SS NCOs came along and attacked us with sticks. We had to form up in rows of five, and it took quite a while, and many blows and insults, before our terrified ranks were assembled. Then we had a roll call, having to step forward and repeat our name and offense, whereupon we were immediately handed over to our particular block leader.

When my name was called I stepped forward, gave my name, and mentioned Paragraph 175. With the words: "You filthy queer, get over there, you butt-fucker!" I received several kicks from behind and was kicked over to an SS sergeant who had charge of my block.

The first thing I got from him was a violent blow on my face that threw me to the ground. I pulled myself up and respectfully stood before him, whereupon he brought his knee up hard into my groin so that I doubled up with pain on the ground. Some prisoners who were on duty immediately called out to me: "Stand up quick, otherwise he'll kick you to bits!"

My face still twisted, I stood up again in front of my block sergeant, who grinned at me and said: "That was your entrance fee, you filthy Viennese swine, so that you know who your block leader is."

When the whole transport was finally divided up, there were about twenty men in our category. We were driven to our block at the double, interrupted by the commands: "Lie down! Stand up! Lie down, stand up!" and so on, from the block leader and some of his men, then having once again to form up in ranks of three. We then had to strip completely naked, lay our clothes on the ground in front of us, with shoes and socks on top, and wait—wait—wait.

It was January and a few degrees below zero, with an icy wind blowing through the camp, yet we were left naked and barefoot on the snow-covered ground, to stand and wait. An SS corporal in winter coat with fur collar strode through our ranks and struck now one of us, now another, with a horse-whip, crying: "This is so you don't make me feel cold, you filthy queers."

He also trod deliberately on the prisoners' toes with his heavy boots, making them cry out in pain. Anyone who made a sound, however, was immediately punched in the stomach with the butt end of his whip with a force that took his breath away. Almost sweating from dealing out blows up and down, the SS corporal said, "You queers are going to remain here until you cool off."[1]

Finally, after a terribly long time, we were allowed to march to the showers—still naked and barefoot. Our clothes, which had already had nametags put in, remained behind, and had vanished when we returned. We had to wash ourselves in cold water, and some of the new arrivals collapsed with cold and exhaustion. Only then did the camp doctor have the warm water turned on, so that we could thaw ourselves out. After the shower we were taken to the next room, where we had to cut our hair, pubic hair included.

---

1   The slang word for homosexual used here is *warmer Bruder*, literally "hot brother," which gives occasion for a lot of vicious puns.

Finally we were taken, still naked—to the clothing stores, where we were given underwear and were "fitted" with prison clothing. This was distributed quite irrespective of size. The trousers I received were far too short, and came only just below my calves; the jacket was much too narrow and had too-short sleeves. Only the coat fitted tolerably well, but by mere accident. The shoes were a little too big and smelled strongly of sweat, but they had leather soles, which made walking a lot easier than the wooden-soled shoes that many new arrivals received. As far as clothing went, at least, I didn't do too badly. Then we had to form up again outside our block and have its organization explained to us by the camp commander. Our block was occupied only by homosexuals, with about 250 men in each wing. We could only sleep in our nightshirts, and had to keep our hands outside the blankets, for: "You queer assholes aren't going to start jerking off here!"

The windows had a centimeter of ice on them. Anyone found with his underclothes on in bed or his hands under his blanket—there were checks almost every night—was taken outside and had several bowls of water poured over him before being left standing outside for a good hour. Only a few people survived this treatment. The least result was bronchitis, and it was rare for any gay person taken into the sick bay to come out alive. We who wore the pink triangle were prioritized for medical experiments, and these generally ended in death. For my part, therefore, I took every care I could not to offend against the regulations.

Our block senior and his aides were "greens"—that is, criminals. They looked it, and behaved like it too. Brutal and merciless toward us "queers," and concerned only with their own privilege and advantage, they were as much feared by us as the SS.

In Sachsenhausen, at least, a homosexual was never permitted to have any position of responsibility. Nor could we even speak with prisoners from other blocks, with a different-colored badge; we were told we might try to seduce them. And yet homosexuality was much more rife in the other blocks, where there were no men with the pink triangle, than it was in our own.

We were also forbidden to approach nearer than five meters of the other blocks. Anyone caught doing so was whipped on the "horse," and was sure of at least fifteen to twenty strokes. Other categories of prisoner were similarly forbidden to enter our block. We were to remain isolated as the damnedest of the damned, the camp's "shitty queers," condemned to liquidation and helpless prey to all the torments inflicted by the SS and the Capos.

The day regularly began at 6 a.m., or 5 a.m. in summer, and in just half an hour we had to be washed, dressed, and have our beds made in the military style. If you still had time, you could have breakfast, which meant hurriedly slurping down the thin flour soup, hot or lukewarm, and eating your piece of bread. Then we had to form up in eights on the parade ground for morning roll call. Work followed, in winter from 7:30 a.m. to 5 p.m., and in summer from 7 a.m. to 8 p.m., with a half-hour break at the workplace. After work, straight back to the camp and immediate parade for evening roll call.

Each block marched in formation to the parade ground and had its permanent position there. The morning parade was not so drawn out as the much-feared evening roll call, for only the block numbers were counted, which took about an hour, and then the command was given for work detachments to form up.

At every parade, those who had just died had also to be present; that is, they were laid out at the end of each block

and counted as well. Only after the parade, having been tal-
lied by the report officer, were they taken to the mortuary and
subsequently burned.

Disabled prisoners had also to be present for parade. Time
and again we helped or carried comrades to the parade
ground who had been beaten by the SS only hours before. Or
we had to bring along fellow prisoners who were half-frozen
or feverish, so as to have our numbers complete. Any man
missing from our block meant many blows and thus further
deaths.

We new arrivals were now assigned to our work, which
was to keep the area around the block clean. That at least
is what we were told by the NCO in charge. In reality, the
purpose was to break the very last spark of independent spirit
that might possibly remain in the new prisoners, by senseless
yet very heavy labor, and to destroy the little human dignity
that we still retained. This work continued until a new batch
of pink-triangle prisoners were delivered to our block and we
were replaced.

Our work, then, was as follows: In the morning we had
to cart the snow outside our block from the left side of the
road to the right side. In the afternoon we had to cart the
same snow back from the right side to the left. We didn't have
barrows and shovels to perform this work either—that would
have been far too simple for us "queers." No, our SS masters
had thought up something much better.

We had to put on our coats with the buttoned side back-
ward, and take the snow away in the container this provided.
We had to shovel up the snow with our hands—our bare
hands, as we didn't have any gloves. We worked in teams of
two. Twenty turns at shoveling up the snow with our hands,
then twenty turns at carrying it away. And so right through
to the evening, and all at the double!

This mental and bodily torment lasted six days, until at last new pink-triangle prisoners were delivered to our block and took over from us. Our hands were cracked all over and half frozen off, and we had become dumb and indifferent slaves of the SS.

I learned from prisoners who had already been in our block a good while that in summer similar work was done with earth and sand.

Above the gate of the prison camp, however, the "meaningful" Nazi slogan was written in big capitals: "Freedom through work!"

3

A CAMP OF TORTURE AND TOIL

AFTER THE INFAMOUS snow detachment, we new arrivals were transferred to the same work as the rest of our entire block: the clay pit of the Klinker brickworks. This clay pit, known among us prisoners as the death pit, was both famed and feared by all prisoners in all other concentration camps, as a factory of human destruction, and up until 1942 it was the "Auschwitz" for homosexuals. Only we were commandeered for work in the clay pit, to be hounded to death by the most terrible working conditions, as well as by actual torture.

Thousands upon thousands of homosexuals must have lost their tormented lives there, victims of a deliberate operation of destruction by the Hitler regime. And yet till this very day no one has come forward to describe this and honor its victims. It seems that "good taste" nowadays prevents people from speaking of the destruction of concentration-camp victims, particularly when these were homosexuals.

Work in the clay pit was the hardest it is possible to imagine, and exposed to all the elements. Whether in summer, with singeing heat, or in winter with biting frost and deep snow, a fixed daily number of carts filled with clay had to be pushed by hand up to the brick-making machines and their ovens, so that sufficient raw material was always available and production need not be interrupted. Since the clay pit was quite deep, the stretch up which these carts had to be hand-pushed on rails to the plant was both very long and very steep. For half-starved prisoners covered with marl, this was a real Golgotha.

The Capos who had immediate supervision over us were strictly ordered by the SS to spare no pains, which meant spare no human life, to get the prescribed tonnage of clay to the brickworks on time. They used this power of life and death with sadistic cruelty, since they were themselves threatened with relegation to the same labor column if the daily quota was not achieved. It is not hard to imagine the brutality they inflicted on the prisoners in their charge, so as not to fall into the same state of toil.

Five or six prisoners had to load the carts with shovels, while other groups of the same size pushed the full carts uphill. The Capos and SS rained almost constant blows on us, hoping to accelerate the work in this way, but also giving free vent to their sadistic impulses. It was no wonder that almost each day some prisoners deliberately got their fingers or toes, even hands or feet, run over by the carts, so as to escape from work in the clay pit. Yet even if they all were sent to the sick bay, they were never seen alive and well again. They just went to fuel the constant flow of human guinea pigs for "medical" research.

It happened very often that the prisoners shoving a full cart uphill simply ran out of strength, and the cart slipped violently back down on them. If it could not be braked in time with wooden sticks, then it ran right back with full force into the cart below. Many prisoners were already so numbed and indifferent that they didn't even bother to jump out of the way when a full cart came roaring toward them. Then human bodies would fly through the air, and limbs be crushed to pulp, while the remaining prisoners only received more blows with the stick. The clay pit thus took its daily toll of fatalities, both accident victims and those who simply succumbed to exhaustion. The death pit richly deserved its name.

My dormitory, with 180 prisoners or more, contained the most varied collection of people. Unskilled workers and shop assistants, skilled tradesmen and independent crafts-men, musicians and artists, professors and clergy, even aristocratic landowners. All of them, before their imprisonment in concentration camps, had been decent people in private life, many indeed highly respected citizens, who had never come up against the law, but were set apart only by their homosexual feelings. All of these otherwise decent people had been assembled here, in this melting pot of disgrace and torment, the "queer block" of a concentration camp, for extermination through back-breaking labor, hunger, and torture. None of them were child molesters or had had sex with children or adolescents, as all of these had a green triangle. Were we with our pink triangle really outrageous criminals and "degenerates," a menace to society?

One of my fellow prisoners, still recognizable as an intellectual despite his battered face and clay-spattered body, was a Jew as well. Beneath the pink triangle he wore the yellow triangle, so that the two together made a star of David. He had to suffer twice-over the chicanery of the SS and the "green" Capos, for being not only queer, but a Jew into the bargain.

He was from Berlin, twenty-five years old at the time, and came from a very well-to-do family. His parents, whose only son he was, had already long since been liquidated in some camp or other, after agreeing that their property in Germany should be "safeguarded" by the Reich. A farce, given that the Nazis would have confiscated all they had anyway.

The son, however, still had significant property in Switzerland and Portugal, and had inherited more besides. He wanted to buy his way out, and was willing to turn over half his fortune to the Nazis in return for permission to emigrate.

His lawyer, however, based in Switzerland, would only transfer the bank accounts and papers to him personally in Zurich, even though German officials endowed with full authority were negotiating the deal. The Swiss lawyer, however, knew the kind of people he was dealing with, and completely refused to agree to the property being transferred to his client in Germany. He wanted to prevent this money, too, being "safeguarded" by the Nazis, while his client remained in concentration camp. In this way he carried on fighting for his client's life and fortune: money only in return for emigration.

Our SS block leader must have got wind of these proceedings, and was well aware that "his" Jewish queer had an enormous fortune abroad. After evening roll call, during what little free time remained to the prisoners, and very often even at night, he would send for "his" Jew and make him stand for a couple of hours in the snow, or make him do dozens upon dozens of knee-bends in the icy cold in his nightshirt, until the poor devil collapsed of exhaustion and passed out.

Then the SS man would lift him up and tell him he should make over to him a portion of his property abroad and notify the Swiss lawyer accordingly. If he did this, he would then leave him in peace and get him a cushy job in domestic work.

But the Berlin Jew never gave in, even though this only meant he was hounded and tortured still more. "I mustn't sign anything. If I do, they'll just kill me, so that I can't be a witness to the extortion," he once said as he told me of his life. "But as long as the SS man hopes that I might give in, he'll carry on torturing me, but he'll at least keep me alive. And I want to live!"

Fourteen days more he had to bear the torment and torture of the SS sergeant. Falling from one faint into another, a

mental and physical wreck, he stubbornly refused to sign anything, as this would have meant certain death. Then suddenly
his torture was ended, he was fetched and taken away by the
Gestapo. It seemed that his Swiss lawyer's negotiations had
been successful—at least that was my fervent wish—and that
the deal of Jew against money had finally taken place.

Money doesn't stink, so our Nazi champions of race in
Berlin would have said, even Jewish money—and "queer" into
the bargain.

For all the deaths and mutilations in the clay pit, the number
of prisoners in our block continued to rise. Almost every week
new transports arrived, each time including a group of gays
who had to be quartered in our block. It was noticeable that the
majority of these new arrivals were Austrians or Sudeten Germans. It seemed that action was under way in these new "German districts" to cleanse them of "degenerate" homosexuals.

Toward the end of February 1940 a priest arrived in our
block, a man some sixty years of age, tall and with distinguished features. We later discovered that he came from
Sudetenland, from an aristocratic German family.

He found the torment of the arrival procedure especially
trying, particularly the long wait naked and barefoot outside
the block. When his tonsure was discovered after the shower,
the SS corporal in charge took up a razor and said, "I'll go to
work on this one's head myself, and extend his tonsure a bit."
And he shaved the priest's head with the razor, taking little
trouble to avoid cutting the scalp. Quite the contrary.

The priest returned to the dayroom of our block with his
head cut open and blood streaming down. His face was ashen
and his eyes stared uncomprehendingly into the distance. He
sat down on a bench, folded his hands in his lap, and said
softly, more to himself than to anyone else: "And yet man is
good, he is a creature of God!"

I was sitting beside him, and said softly but firmly: "Nor all men; there are also beasts in human form, whom the devil must have made."

The priest paid no attention to my words; he just prayed silently, merely moving his lips. I was deeply moved, even though I was by then already numbed by all the suffering I had so often seen, and indeed experienced myself. But I had always had a great respect for priests, so that his silent prayer, this mute appeal to God, whom he called on for help and strength in his bodily pain and mental torment, went straight to my heart.

Our block Capo, however, a repulsive and brutal "green," must have reported the priest's praying to the SS, for our block sergeant suddenly burst into the dayroom accompanied by a second NCO, seizing the terrified priest from the bench and punching and insulting him. The priest bore the beating and abuse without complaint, and just stared at the two SS men with wide, astonished eyes. This must simply have made them angrier, for they now took one of the benches and tied the priest to it.

They started to beat him indiscriminately with their sticks, on his stomach, his belly, and his sexual organs. They seemed to get more and more ecstatic, and gloated: "We'll drive the praying out of you! You butt-fucker! Butt-fucker!"

The priest collapsed into unconsciousness, was shaken awake, and then fell unconscious again.

Finally the two SS sadists ceased their blows and left the dayroom, though not without scornfully calling back to the man they had now quite destroyed: "Okay, you randy old rat-bag, you can piss with your asshole in future."

The priest just rattled and groaned. We released him and laid him on his bed. He tried to raise his hand in thanks, but he hadn't the strength, and his voice gave out when he tried to say thank you. He just lay without stirring, his eyes open, each movement contorting his face with pain.

I felt I was witnessing the crucifixion of Christ in modern guise. Instead of Roman soldiers, Hitler's SS thugs, and a bench instead of the cross. The torment of the Savior, however, was scarcely greater than that inflicted on one of his representatives nineteen hundred years later here in Sachsenhausen.

The next morning, when we marched to the parade ground, we had almost to carry the priest, who seemed about to collapse again from pain and weakness. When our block senior reported to the SS block sergeant, the latter came over to the priest and shouted: "Can't you stand up, you asshole?" adding: "You filthy queer, you filthy swine, say what you are!" The priest was supposed to repeat the insults, but no sound came from the lips of the broken man. The SS man angrily fell on him and was about to start beating him once again.

Suddenly the unimaginable happened, something that is still inexplicable to me and that I could only see as a miracle, the finger of God: From the overcast sky, a sudden ray of sunshine illuminated the priest's battered face.

Out of thousands of assembled prisoners, it lit only him, and at the very moment when he was going to be beaten again. There was a remarkable silence, and all present stared fixedly at the sky, astonished by what had happened. The SS sergeant himself looked up at the clouds in wonder for a few seconds, then let his hand, raised for a beating, sink slowly to his side, and walked wordlessly away to take up his position at the end of our ranks.

The priest bowed his head and murmured with a dying voice: "Thank you, Lord ... I know that my time has come ..."

He was still with us for the evening parade. But we no longer needed to carry him: we laid him down at the end of the line with the other dead of the day, so that our numbers should be complete for the roll call—no matter whether living or dead.

By now it was April, yet I was still alive, despite constant work in the clay pit.

Though already weak in my body, my mind was still absolutely clear and alert. A necessary condition, if one was to remain alive in concentration camp and survive the incessant torment.

One day I was called out at morning parade and transferred to a different work detachment, assigned to build a new firing range for the SS.

God, how happy I was to get out of the death pit! An end to the daily beatings of the Capos, an end to seeing the daily mutilation of my fellow prisoners, my tormented and despairing companions in pain. At last a different kind of work.

My joy, unfortunately, was brief and soon cut short, for it turned out that I had only exchanged the frying pan for the fire. Once again, it was only homosexuals who were employed, plus a few Jews who never returned to the camp in the evening alive. I soon found out how in this unit too, no concern was shown for human life, particularly the lives of queers and Jews.

We had to carry earth and clay to build up a mound for the firing-range butts, to stand behind the target zone, which was already installed. At first this went off quite smoothly; we carted our barrows and the earth wall slowly rose. But then, after only a few days, groups of SS men came to the firing range to start their shooting practice, while we prisoners had to carry on emptying our barrows onto the mound. Naturally enough, we wanted to stop unloading when the shooting practice was going on, but the Capos and SS guards forced us to continue with blows and threats of a beating.

Then shots started to whip through our ranks, and several of my fellow sufferers collapsed, some only wounded, but many killed.

We soon found out that the SS far preferred to fire on us prisoners than they did at the proper targets, and had directly aimed at certain people pushing their barrows.

Every day, our group suffered some dead and wounded. We came to work each morning full of terror and dread, not knowing which of us were to meet our death, but sure that some or other of us would. We had become a sitting target for the SS, who greeted each direct hit with a shout of glee.

This lasted almost two weeks, and claimed more than fifteen dead—dead prisoners with the pink triangle—more victims, in fact, than the notorious clay pit claimed in the same time, even though the number of prisoners working there was far greater.

In this way the SS's demonic machinery of extermination ravaged the ranks of us gays, pruning the numbers in our block only to make way for the next batch of homosexuals sent in from the Reich and its newly occupied territories.

The command of the Nazi regime for a drastic purge of homosexuals, these "degenerates" among the German people who were to be dispatched for extermination, was carried out by the SS jailers efficiently and with sadistic zeal. But the intention was not just to kill us off immediately, but rather to torture us to death by a combination of terror and brutality, hunger and bitter toil.

It must have been great sport for the SS, then, to use us pink-triangle prisoners as living targets. What a nice change for them, to have live human beings to play with!

For two whole days I came through the rain of bullets miraculously unscathed. Then one of the Capos, a "green," offered me a bargain. I need only load earth into the barrows, and not carry them to the butts, if I would be his lover and have sex with him. Then I'd no longer be exposed to the shots of the SS.

Quickly thinking it over, I agreed, for my will to live was now stronger than my commitment to human decency. No matter who might condemn me for it, the sight of the dead and wounded at the firing range had had too great an effect on me. I was afraid, terribly afraid. Why shouldn't I seize this opportunity to save my life, even if it was degrading?

On May 15, 1940, at morning parade, a transport was put together, quite unexpectedly, for transfer to another camp. I was to go with it, and scarcely an hour later we were loaded onto a truck and driven away. In some ways I was sorry to go, for in the last few weeks my life had been almost bearable, through this sexual relationship with my Capo. He got more for me to eat, and thanks to his help I was assigned only to easier and nondangerous work.

Departure from my Capo friend was brief and painless. We shook hands, he said, "I'm sorry for you," and I thanked him. A relationship of convenience on both sides was at an end.

With anxious feelings, I boarded the truck, not knowing what the future would bring, and how I would survive in the new camp. Experience, however, had taught me that it was possible to keep alive even in concentration camp. And I was obsessed by a single thought: that I was determined to survive.

4

FLOSSENBÜRG

IT WAS ONLY during the journey that we learned from the SS guards that we were being taken to Flossenbürg. I had already heard tell of that camp from other prisoners in Sachsenhausen. According to them, things were just as brutal in Flossenbürg as at Sachsenhausen, so we need have no hopes that we were in for any better times. In that respect, one concentration camp was as bad as another.

Flossenbürg lay in the mountainous region of Bavaria, near the Czech border, at about 700 meters above sea level. The nearest town was Weiden. The concentration camp was built on a gentle slope, not far from Flossenbürg village. But no matter how scenically beautiful, with a ruined fourteenth-century castle rising picturesquely in the landscape, Flossenbürg is still a place of dreaded memory for tens of thousands of human beings, and for their pain and torment there they will curse it for all time.

When our transport of three trucks arrived in Flossenbürg, and we were unloaded onto the parade ground, we were surprised to find that we didn't face the same circus that was customary for new arrivals in Sachsenhausen—that is, abuse, insults, and blows. Our arrival, at least, seemed more "civilized," which was a pleasant experience.

Out of over a hundred Sachsenhausen prisoners transferred to Flossenbürg, only five bore the pink triangle: a
Czech singer from Prague, age 35; a civil servant from Graz
in Austria, age 42; a 24-year-old man from Salzburg, said to
have been a senior official in the Hitler Youth; myself, and
another Viennese, both aged 22. Just as in Sachsenhausen, we
were quartered in a "queers' block," but this time only wing A
of the block—that is, one dormitory—was for homosexuals.

This wing alone was occupied by more than two hundred
men, and here too, as in Sachsenhausen, the light was kept
on the whole night, though only in the "queers' wing" of the
block. Once again, we had to keep our hands outside the
blanket while we slept. This was presumably a regulation in
force for all concentration camps with blocks for homosexuals. Only a year later, when this wing was disbanded and we
were scattered in smaller groups throughout the other blocks,
was this regulation no longer applied.

We were led to our block by an SS guard, and transferred
there to the sergeant in charge. This man kept us standing
and waiting for a good while, while a group of eight to ten
Capos gathered round us and looked us up and down. I was
already wise enough to know exactly why a section of the
"dignitaries"—who included the Capos—were admiring us in
this way. They were on the lookout for a possible lover among
the new arrivals. Because I still did not have a full beard, even
though nearly twenty-three, so looked younger than my years,
and because I had filled out a bit again thanks to the supple-
mentary rations from my Sachsenhausen Capo, I was obviously very much at the center of these Capos' considerations.
I could tell as much from their unconcealed discussions. The
situation in which the five of us found ourselves seemed to me
very much like a slave-boy market in ancient Rome.

In the end the SS sergeant and the block senior came out of the block office and put an end to the Capos' game. While the sergeant read us out the special regulations for the homosexual wing of the block, the block senior stood behind him and took a good look at us, with the same idea in mind as his Capos had had before. His eyes stayed fixed on me for a good while, and a contented smile appeared on his face. When the sergeant had departed, and the block senior had to assign us new arrivals our beds, he immediately came up to me and said, "Hey, you, kid, do you want to come with me?"

"Yes, certainly," I said right away, knowing very well what he meant. My immediate acceptance somehow made an impression on him. He said, "You're a clever kid, I like that," and patted me on the shoulder. Flossenbürg was a camp run by the "greens," just like Sachsenhausen. The great majority of elders and Capos, in other words, came from the ranks of the criminal prisoners, as naturally enough did the camp senior and head Capo.

The senior whose lover I became was a professional criminal from Hamburg, very highly regarded in his milieu as a safecracker. He was much feared by the prisoners for his ruthlessness, and even by his Capo colleagues, but he was generous and considerate to me. Only half a year later he became camp senior, and remained so until the Americans liberated the camp. Even later on, when I was no longer his lover, his eye having fallen on a young Pole, he kept a protecting hand over me. He saved my life more than ten times over, and I am still very grateful to him for this today, more than twenty-five years later. He is once again living in Hamburg, though I have had no contact with him since April 1945.

I was told by my fellow prisoners here that our SS block sergeant was very "sharp," immediately ready with punishments, and never smiling or showing any emotion, but never laying a hand on a prisoner himself. After the five of us new arrivals had made our beds in the prescribed fashion and put our modest belongings away in the appropriate place, we had to parade again for our personal details to be taken down. The sergeant used a pen of one of the prisoners to write down these particulars, asking each of us every possible question.

When it came to my turn and he looked me in the eyes, it was as if a flicker of understanding flashed from him to me. I can't find the right words to express it, but it was like an electric shock that I seemed to feel as we looked at one another those few seconds. He never spoke to me much while I was in his block, but I often found him gazing at me.

Once, when an SS corporal struck me for not taking my cap off to him in time, he burst out of his office and cried, "Leave that man alone!"

Whereupon the corporal left off, saying, "Okay then, okay," and made his departure. The sergeant stared at me with a serious expression and went back into his office. Time and again I caught him looking in my direction when he thought he was unobserved. I never discussed this with any of my fellow prisoners, not even with my friend the block senior, but I had the instinctive feeling that he was fond of me, and also "one of us," of the same sexual persuasion as we who wore the pink triangle.

He concealed his feelings by rejecting any personal contact with us prisoners, and by his strictness and rigidity. For even the slightest infringement of camp regulations, and that might mean as little as a cough at the wrong time or a button missing, he would order five to ten strokes on the "horse," the customary penalty. But he never watched the punishment himself, and on one occasion when he had to be present, he turned away. In mid-1941 he volunteered for the Russian front and vanished from our sight.

We gays were assembled into work detachments of twelve to fifteen men, led by an SS work leader, a Capo, and a foreman, to work in the granite quarry. This is where the stones were dug and prepared for Hitler's great building projects, for roadway bridges and the like. Great halls were dug into the quarry, where the cutting and finishing of the stones was carried out, and the granite blocks received their final form and possible polishing.

The work of quarrying, dynamiting, hewing, and dressing was extremely arduous, and only Jews and homosexuals were assigned to it. The quarry claimed very many victims, with the SS and Capos often deliberately contributing to the large number of accidents.

What car driver today, hurtling along the German roadways, knows that each block of granite has the blood of innocent men on it? Men who did nothing wrong, but who were hounded to death in concentration camps solely for reason of their religion, their origin, their political views, or their feeling for their own sex. Each of the granite pillars that hold up the roadway bridges cost the lives of untold victims—a sea of blood and a mountain of human corpses. Today people are only too willing to throw a cloak of silence and forgetfulness over all of these things.

Because of my relationship with the block senior, the Capo in charge assigned me to somewhat easier work in the quarry, though this was still hard enough. And I could not have kept up the heavy work day after day if my friend had not procured me additional rations.

Just like the prison camp itself, the granite quarry was completely surrounded by barbed wire, and guarded outside and inside by SS sentries. No prisoner was permitted to get closer than five meters to the wire. Anyone who did so was shot by the SS guards without warning, since this transgression was already considered attempted escape. For shooting a prisoner who "attempted escape," an SS man received three days' special leave.

It is not hard to imagine, therefore, how keen the SS were to organize "escapes" of this kind, for the sake of their extra leave. In the relatively short time that I worked in the quarry, I myself witnessed at least ten occasions when SS men seized a prisoner's cap and threw it against the wire. They would then demand that the prisoner fetch his cap back. Naturally enough, the prisoner tried to refuse, as everyone knew this meant certain death. The SS men then started beating the poor devil with sticks, so that he could only choose the way in which he was to die: either be beaten to death by the SS beasts or be shot by the guards for "attempted escape."

It happened several times, too, that a prisoner would himself run against the wire in despair, to get shot and be freed from pain, hunger, and the unbearable toil.

When a prisoner was shot in the quarry, all other prisoners had immediately to lie on the ground and keep their heads down, until the victim, who was not always immediately dead, was taken away on a stretcher. This might take anything up to an hour and a half. Anyone who moved, moreover, got a kick in the head or the kidneys from the patrolling SS guards, so that he nearly lost his senses. Only in summer was this procedure relatively bearable; in rain or on cold days it was more than painful, which was precisely the SS's idea.

One way of tormenting Jews and homosexuals that the SS in the quarry were very fond of was to drive crazy prisoners who were already physically at the end of their tether. A man who had not done anything in particular, but was simply picked upon by the SS officer in charge, would have a metal bucket placed over his head. Two men would hold him down, while the SS men and Capos banged on the bucket with their sticks. The terrible noise amplified through the bucket soon brought the victim to such a pitch of terror that he completely lost his mind and his sense of balance was destroyed. Then the bucket was suddenly removed from his head and he was pushed toward the wire fence. He could seldom right himself in time. And if he staggered inside the 5-meter zone, he was fired on in the usual way. "Games" such as these were a favorite pastime for some of the SS guards, who had no need to fear any disciplinary measures, their victims being just the homosexuals and Jews whose extermination was planned for in any case.

After two weeks or so in the quarry, I was assigned to a different work detachment at the instigation of my block senior friend. This was the camp's building division, in charge of all construction work in the Flossenbürg area, whether within or outside of the camp itself. The building division had several work detachments, one for each of the different building sites. I was to work as a clerk in the building material stores, and so had an easy and comfortable job that no longer put my life in daily jeopardy. At last I'd come through!

The only reason I was given this position was that I had passed my "probation" period as the block senior's lover, and without attracting attention. What was on trial was not the sincerity of the relationship, but my silence and discretion about it.

If my lover was feared among the "dignitaries," he was also respected, and as these were almost exclusively "greens"—that is, criminals—he was a kind of underworld boss. He had very good relations with the SS camp commanders and officers, keeping on good terms with them by way of little presents. These were generally handicraft items made by the prisoners, such as Viking ships, painted or in bottles, watercolors, straw baskets, and wickerwork of various kinds, which he got made in return for cigarettes or little packets of food. These products of prison handicraft were very popular with the SS, as they could also be sold at a good price outside the camp. In this way, then, my block senior managed to purchase the favor of many SS officers, and built up a position of power both among the ordinary prisoners and among his Capo colleagues. His influence was so great that at the end of 1940, as I already mentioned, the SS appointed him to be camp senior.

Naturally enough, he also had his enemies, particularly among the politicals, who would have liked to have got the position for themselves. In these first days of my friendship with him, therefore, some "reds"—that is, political prisoners—approached me in the quarry even though they lived in another block and belonged to another work detachment. They wanted to find out what there was between me and the block senior, how he treated me, and whether he had approached me sexually. They put these questions to me in the form of jokes, for example, "Has he got a big one?"; "Does he give it to you every day?"; "Is he really loving?"

The only purpose of these jokes, however, was to bring to light a homosexual relationship that was officially forbidden. As later emerged, their idea was to overthrow the block senior in this way and put an end to his influence in the camp. The "greens" would then lose their positions to the "reds."

I never let anything slip or gave any indication that there was anything "between us," simply answering their ironic questions with: "Ask him yourself, I don't know anything about it." For what I did know very well is that if I gave away even the least thing about our relationship, I would be torn to pieces in the power struggle between reds and greens. Any homosexual relationship could bring very severe punishment to both parties, generally leading to death. At least this was the case in 1940; later on camp morals were a little bit more relaxed.

My block senior, of course, knew all about the attempt to deprive him of his position and chance of promotion—and also about my obstinate silence as to our relationship. He was happy to use his connections and arrange for me to be assigned to a desk job in the building material stores, even though positions of this kind were in general quite taboo for prisoners with the pink triangle.

"You're a sticker, kid," he told me generously, with a slap on the shoulders. "I like that, and I like you still more for it, even though I'd rather have a bird."

By "sticker," he meant that I kept my mouth shut and didn't give anything away, even under threat. His rough confession of love, even with the rider that he preferred women, somehow made me happy and met my need for protection. From then on I was very attached to him.

When a prisoner was sentenced to be beaten, this was carried out on the "horse," and all prisoners in the block had to attend and witness the punishment. If this was carried out on the parade ground, then all prisoners in the camp had to attend.

The "horse" was a wooden frame, like a bench, to which the prisoner was tied on his stomach, in such a way that his head and torso faced vertically down, his buttocks upward and his legs down the other side. The legs were pulled forward and also secured. Just to be tied to the "horse" was a torture in itself. But what torment when the blows began to fall. The instrument used could vary, either a dogwhip, a stick, or, in most cases, the much-feared horsewhip.

The NCOs who almost invariably carried out the punishment were generally those with the most sadistic disposition, who volunteered to do the job. What we are talking about here, of course, are the official punishments imposed by the camp commanders. Many of the SS block leaders and work detachment leaders, however, keenly delivered their own punishments on the "horse." But then these were not carried out in the open but in the offices and workshops. Frequently a prisoner condemned to be whipped in this way tried to put a second pair of underpants or something similar under his trousers as "protection." If this was noticed, then the punishment was made more severe, and he was whipped on the naked behind.

Once, when a Czech prisoner from my dormitory was caught trying to escape, he was sentenced to twenty-five strokes on the "horse," the highest number that could be given at once. After evening roll call he was tied to the "horse" erected outside our block, and we gays, the whole of wing A, had to stand in rows to witness the punishment. The evening meal was canceled for that day.

The camp commander, an *SS Obersturmführer* of small stature, smooth shaven, and about forty-five years of age, was a repulsive beast. If he caught any man with the pink triangle in the slightest infringement of regulations, he sentenced him to punishment on the "horse." At least every second day there was a procedure of this kind outside our block, at which he was always personally present.

When the Czech homosexual from my dormitory was tied to the "horse," an SS sergeant who was well known for his beatings appeared with the horsewhip. The lashing was to be inflicted on the Czech's naked buttocks. At every stroke, the offender had to count aloud, and if he did not call the number correctly, out of pain, or not loud enough, then the blow didn't count. It often happened in this way that the victim received almost double the number of blows officially imposed.

When the Czech was being beaten, and screaming and trembling with pain, the SS sergeant cracked his whip through the air. At the very first strokes the Czech's skin had already burst open and started bleeding, but the SS man continued unperturbed, always making sure that his victim called out the numbers loud enough, even if in Czech.

The camp commander stood right by, and looked visibly more than a little interested in the proceedings. At each stroke his eyes lit up, and after a few strokes his whole face was red with excitement. He buried his hands in his trouser pockets and could clearly be seen to masturbate, quite unperturbed by our presence. After satisfying himself in this way, the perverted swine suddenly disappeared, being no longer interested in the further execution of the punishment.

At last the twenty-five strokes had been delivered, but the Czech was still not released from the "horse," and hung there shivering. The SS sergeant commanded the medical Capo who had to be present at each punishment to sprinkle the Czech's bleeding buttocks with iodine, so that the poor devil screamed with pain once again. When he was released, he had to join us in our ranks, still quaking with pain, his trousers stained red with blood from his buttocks and legs. As a further punishment, the whole of wing A, almost two hundred of us, had to stand outside our block until midnight, because one of us had attempted to escape. And that meant standing completely still. Anyone who moved or tried to relieve their exhausted feet got a blow from the SS guards.

I myself witnessed on more than thirty occasions how this camp commander got sexual satisfaction from watching the lashings inflicted on the "horse," and the perverted lust with which he followed each stroke and the screams of the victim. On one occasion there was one of us pink-triangle prisoners who failed to let out a sound while being beaten, even though he was thrashed most forcefully. However hard the SS man hit him, the prisoner kept his lips together. This robbed the commander of part of his fun, so he shouted at the prisoner: "You filthy queer, why aren't you screaming? Perhaps you're enjoying it, you butt-fucker!" "Start again from the beginning," he said, turning to the SS guard, "and go on until the swine starts screaming."

The SS man struck with such force that the victim's skin broke open in centimeter-wide weals at each stroke, and his blood ran down to the ground. Now even the "silent one" saw reason; he howled like an animal and screamed for help—help which we couldn't give him. But the commander was panting with excitement, and masturbated wildly in his trousers until he came.

5

THE POLISH BOYS AND THE GYPSY CAPO

THE FLOSSENBÜRG COMMANDANT, an *SS Ober-sturmbannführer* who was later promoted to *Standartenführer*, gave little attention to the internal management of the prison camp, and left all this to his two camp commanders. Before he joined the *Waffen SS*, he had been an officer in the army. This earlier career might be the reason why he was very correct in his dealings with the prisoners, and showed certain humane tendencies.

His attitude was particularly striking in contrast with the brutal rule of his SS subordinates. As far as I can remember, in all the years that he was commandant he never ordered corporal punishment on the "horse," or attended its execution. He seemed to find the torture of the prisoners by the camp SS, of which he must have known, so unpleasant that he would often not enter the prison camp for weeks at a time. But even if he disliked the inhumane punishment of us prisoners by the SS, he was not prepared to do anything to stop it. Political prisoners, moreover, were a category he particularly disliked, presumably seeing them as very dangerous to the Reich's internal security, which is why he favored the criminals, the "greens," for the management of the prisoners' affairs.

The camp authorities had decided to establish a prisoners' orchestra in Flossenbürg, such as already existed in other concentration camps, and served to "divert" the prisoners on Sundays.

Naturally, we prisoners had to finance the orchestra ourselves, and buy the instruments with our own money. A collection was therefore made. At that time, however, prisoners were officially forbidden to keep any money. What cash a prisoner brought into the camp with him, or received from his relatives and friends, was accounted for on a card. The money itself was kept in the camp safe. Illegally, however, most of the prisoners still kept some money on them, particularly the "dignitaries." Later on, in 1942, each prisoner was permitted to draw thirty marks per month from his account—if he had one—and keep this on him.

When a collection such as this was taken, the prisoners were not asked by the SS whether they wanted to donate money or not; the block leaders simply went through the account cards of their prisoners and determined the "voluntary" contribution in each case by the level of the prisoner's account. In this way, the most surprising sums were accumulated.

One day, a truck filled with musical instruments, straight from the factory, arrived in the camp and was unloaded onto the parade ground. Naturally, not all of the instruments were destined for our orchestra, even though the prisoners had paid for them with their "donations." The SS NCOs first went through and took what they wanted for their own orchestra. As they cynically put it, these were presents from the prisoners to their guards.

The prisoners' orchestra was then put together, and certain people from my dormitory—that is, gays—who happened to be professional musicians, were called in. The members of the orchestra were moved to a special dormitory of their own, where they both lived and practiced, and were sheltered from the tortures of the SS. The singer from Prague, who had been transferred together with me from Sachsenhausen, and with whom I had developed a platonic friendship, was also enrolled in the orchestra.

It was not long before the first concert was given. Everyone in the block had to sit on the floor in the laundry and listen. Attendance was a duty from which no prisoner could be excused; even our entertainment was determined and run by the camp authorities. It didn't matter at all whether a prisoner liked music or, what was rather more common, was not in the mood for it. And what a macabre situation, when the band played sweet songs of happiness, while we prisoners were exposed each day to the torments of the SS! The band could not play Franz Lehár's melodies beautifully enough for anyone to forget for one moment the dreadful situation we were in. That at least was my experience.

The singer from Prague had to sing his operetta numbers, even though he didn't find it at all easy suddenly to sing such happy songs in the midst of the prison-camp misery. But after the first three or four, he was a singer again, and forgot that he was still a prisoner in concentration camp.

He started singing a song from the operetta *The Student Beggar* by Millöcker, "The Polish girl is so pretty . . . ," but suddenly was ordered by the camp commander to break off. "We conquered Poland in war, and it is forbidden to sing of the beauty or attractiveness of the women of a conquered enemy. Only German women are beautiful and attractive."

That was enough!

These concerts for the prisoners were not given all that often, however, for a concentration camp is not a health farm, as the camp commander put it. Certainly no one could challenge that statement. On Sundays, however, the prisoners' orchestra often assembled on the parade ground and played their marches and operetta tunes, as if to present the image of the carefree and easy life in the camp.

At least twice a year we had an official visit. Either the Swedish or Finnish Red Cross sent a representative to the camp. I don't think I am wrong in assuming that the Nazi regime itself invited delegations from Red Cross organizations to visit the concentration camps, so as to give them a picture of their correct management and operation.

Whenever we had such a visit, the orchestra had to play pleasant tunes on the parade ground, while the rest of us had to stroll through the grounds, rather than work. The visitors stood on the watchtower and observed the "peaceful" life of the camp, with no suspicion of how different things were at other times. If they insisted on visiting the prison camp itself, they were generally driven to the headquarters block, where the SS officers' servants lived. This was always kept in particularly good shape, as these people had a lot of free time and could take particular care of their quarters. They were ordered to do so, in fact, so that this shop window was always prepared to receive an official visit.

Visitors were never taken to the Jewish blocks, however, for the ladies and gentlemen from the Red Cross could then have seen how up to three or four men had to lie in one bed, and how they were virtually left to starve. If the visitors wanted to speak to a prisoner, they were introduced to a domestic servant whom the SS had already told in advance what to say. And since this man would want to hang on to his cushy job, and was well aware of the fists of the SS, he said what he was told to. In this way, the real life of the concentration camps, and the sufferings and tortures of the prisoners, were successfully concealed from the international Red Cross. This is presumably why the humanitarian organizations were so outraged about the German camps when they discovered the true situation after the collapse of the Third Reich, as opposed to the pretense that they had accepted on their earlier visits.

In winter 1940–41 we received the first transport from Poland. These Poles had been sent to concentration camp for resisting the German occupation forces or for partisan activities. They ranged from sixteen to sixty years of age, and all looked completely depressed and apathetic. Presumably they had been fearfully mistreated before arriving at Flossenbürg. The authorities were afraid to put them all together, so they were divided up between the various blocks.

After a few days, the block seniors and Capos, or at least the majority of them, all had a young Pole as batman or "cleaner," though the main purpose of these lads was as bed partner for their boss. For the young Poles, however, who were soon almost all disposed of in this way, this situation was far from uncomfortable, for they very quickly realized that without a lover among the "dignitaries" and the extra rations this provided, they would go hungry and have to work as hard as the other prisoners. These young Poles, accordingly, and later young Russians as well, then gladly accepted any proposals that meant both easier work and a full stomach.

These dolly-boys, as they were called in certain other camps, were generally from sixteen to twenty years old. They soon grew to be very cheeky, as they were always protected by their prominent friends, no matter how arrogantly they behaved toward their fellow prisoners. Little could be done against the dolly-boys, for fear of their masters' revenge, and so the cleverest thing was simply to get out of the way. You could soon tell easily from someone's appearance whether he had a relationship with a block senior or Capo. Being properly fed, these young Poles soon grew to be as plump as capons, while thousands of other prisoners in the same camp were starving.

The prisoners with the pink triangle were, as always, "filthy queers" in the eyes of the other prisoners, while the very fellow prisoners who insulted and condemned us in this way were quite unperturbed by relationships that the block seniors and Capos had with the young Poles, and just smiled at this behavior, even if somewhat ironically. This was also the view of many SS officers, who naturally knew all about these relationships with the young Poles, even if nothing was officially said about it.

And so the way a person was assessed by his fellows had two sides to it, as it still unfortunately does today. What in one case is accepted with a smile is completely forbidden when it is openly proclaimed or made public. Homosexual behavior between two "normal" men is considered an emergency outlet, while the same thing between two gay men, who both feel deeply for one another, is something "filthy" and repulsive.

At almost the same time that the Poles arrived in Flossenbürg, my friend the block senior was appointed the new camp senior, LA 1.

Since he had to move to a different block, where the camp office was situated, we had to part, for he certainly couldn't have me, a pink-triangle prisoner, visit him there, and in any case he didn't want to draw attention to himself and give grounds for suspicion that he was a "175er." This would not just have meant his immediate dismissal, but also a heavy punishment for us both.

When he said good-bye, the last time we were together, and explained to me the reasons for our separation, I was very moved and sad. But he assured me that he would always be grateful for my loyalty, above all for my silence, and would still keep an eye on me, also that I could always count on him for help. It was a difficult parting for me, even though our relationship was hardly the most idealistic, but sprang from self-preservation. And yet I was very attached to him for the several times when his aid had saved my life. He continued to help me in the remaining years I was in the camp, whenever I got into trouble or was threatened with punishment. He never broke the promise he gave me when we parted. He remains in my eyes an honorable man, even if he was a safecracker and burglar by trade, and possibly still is today.

Straight after this separation, of course, I received offers from other "green" Capos and block seniors. For not all of these wanted a young Pole as their lover, some finding them either too young or not entertaining enough, since the Polish dolly-boys could only speak their own language, at least at that time. In order to keep my good position as a clerk, and to receive additional food that was necessary to stay alive, I was forced by necessity to enter into a new relationship. It was hardly possible, in fact, to refuse, for the Capos knew about my relationship with the new camp senior, which had lasted several months, and he had told them about my discretion as well as my "valuable services" in bed. On top of this, rejection of such an offer would immediately have brought down on me the hatred of all the Capos and a persecution that would surely have led to my death. So there was no other choice but to place myself once again under the protection of a block senior or Capo, who would fend off other propositions, provide me with additional rations, and also make sure that I kept my desk job. In return I had to be lover and bed partner at any time when my protector had the desire. Everything has its price.

My new relationship began not without complication. Three Capos, in fact, wanted me as a lover, and spent a lot of time arguing about the matter. Naturally, I had no choice whatsoever, being quite powerless. I was just told: "One of us will be your new friend," and waited anxiously to see who I would fall to as "booty."

The "struggle" lasted two days, then in the evening a Capo from my building division revealed that he had won me and would be my new lover. He was a Hungarian Gypsy, and also well known among all the prisoners, including the seniors and even the SS, as a petty trader. He carried on regular commerce with the camp kitchen, the sick bay, and the clothing stores. You could buy from him equally a loaf of bread, a diamond ring, or a good pair of shoes. He always had more than enough money. In order to acquire me as his lover, he simply paid off his two rivals, and once a suitable sum was agreed, all parties were satisfied.

Scarcely thirty years of age, this Hungarian was a real *"Feschak,"* as we say in Vienna, a handsome man, tall, thin, and in good physical shape, even after two years in concentration camp. His hair was visibly coal black despite the prison shearing, and he had full lips and dark eyes, blazing with fire when he made love, burning with hate when he was jealous—and he was always jealous of anyone who spoke to me. After only a few days he was already madly in love with me, and met every wish that I uttered in terms of clothing or food.

He had regular dealings with prisoners who worked in the clothing stores. Since new arrivals had to leave their clothes without warning to go naked into the showers, and were then fitted with their prison uniforms without getting their original clothing back, most often the clothing received in the stores turned out to have money or jewelry sewn into it. The SS, of course, were well aware of this, and they were the first to go through this clothing for hidden valuables. But they were generally fairly hasty in this, as none of them wanted to be caught out by a superior and have to hand in what they had found. The prisoners working in the clothing stores could thus still find a good deal of hidden money and jewelry, which they used to buy additional food and alcohol. Both these items they purchased from my friend the Gypsy.

You really could even buy alcohol from him. Since he was always employed in an outside work detachment, that is, outside the camp perimeter—for there was always building work or painting to be done on the houses of the SS—he often had contact with the local civilian population. Though he never told me as much, it seems that he operated in partnership with the sergeant in charge of his work detachment, for he could always obtain a few liters of corn liquor from some civilians in return for a high enough price. The major problem was how to get through the camp gate with it, for every returning prisoner was strictly checked by the guards to see that he didn't bring in anything forbidden.

But my Capo friend didn't find it hard to smuggle in alcohol. Most usually, he used galvanized water pipes that were needed by the building division, in general three to five meters long. A few days before, he would have a few pipes brought out to where his detachment was working. There the pipes would be cleaned and filled, and then sealed in such a way that the corks were at least 20 centimeters from the end of the pipe. The corks could only be seen, then, if the pipes were very closely examined. These were brought back into the camp in the evening, and put down at the gate when the prisoners were examined. When the command was given to enter, the pipes were simply picked up again by the prisoners, who of course were in on the deal, and dropped off at the building material stores, where the alcohol was subsequently extracted.

My new friend was never short of ideas when it came to making money out of nothing. Where money was concerned he thought only of himself, though also of me when money was not. His work detachment, involved with him in the alcohol smuggling, he held together by the threat that he would kill anyone who betrayed him to the SS. He never was betrayed, and continued his alcohol business unmolested.

On the other hand, the Gypsy gave his smuggling team a good share in the proceeds, and was never brutal or slap-happy. So he never gave any prisoner on his team a reason for turning against him. His motto was: Live and let live. His team knew this, and kept an iron discipline. They also knew that he did business with many SS men, and could easily have any of them got rid of if they let anything slip. This group was ruled by a combination of fear and greed; that was the bond that held it together.

From my desk in the building division stores I had a good clear view out onto the parade ground and across to the watchtower, and could observe very well what was going on there. If the SS sentries came out of their guardroom and formed up in rows, that was a sure sign the camp commandant was about to arrive at the prisoners' camp for an inspection. I could also see very clearly the offices of the camp commanders, so I could tell when they were about to start their patrol through the camp. On top of that, I could observe very closely when anyone was put in the arrest cells, the bunker, as well as all new arrivals at the camp. This was extremely interesting, and satisfied my curiosity.

At the end of February 1941, I saw one day from the window of my office a police wagon drive through the camp gate and come to a halt just outside the individual cells in the bunker. These individual cells were used as arrest cells for special punishment. An *SS Obersturmbannführer* in full uniform stepped out, dripping with silver ribbons and decorations, together with an elegant young lady in shimmering evening dress, and revealing a snow white shoulder. She was very made-up and wore silver shoes with high heels.

At first I thought that the SS officer and his lady had had a breakdown, and had continued here with the police wagon for their inspection of the camp. But when they were both locked into individual cells in the bunker building, and the police wagon drove off again, I was eager to find out more. In the evening I immediately told my Capo friend of these strange new arrivals, and he showed great interest, particularly in the lady's jewelry. I didn't find that surprising, as I was already familiar with his talent for "organizing."

The same evening I learned from my friend, who had already found out everything about the couple, that they had been arrested in a box at the Hamburg opera, following a denunciation, and immediately brought to Flossenbürg.

The *SS Obersturmbannführer* was an officer at the front, with many decorations, including the Knight's Cross, which I hadn't been able to see when he was brought in. His lady turned out to be a young man of nineteen, a soldier in the *Waffen SS* and home on leave in Hamburg. He was the son of one of the biggest and richest nightclub magnates on the Reeperbahn.

They remained in their separate cells until the camp was liberated in April 1945, and were never allowed out the whole day long. Later I discovered that each of them was allowed out for an hour at night, separately of course, to breathe fresh air and stretch their legs. They were kept in those cells, without trial, at the express command of *SS Reichsführer* Heinrich Himmler, cut off from the whole world, even the world of the concentration camp, for the SS didn't want such a prominent officer from the front to mix with the other prisoners and have to wear a badge—let alone the most despised badge of all, the pink triangle of the homosexuals. They were ashamed, and certainly put out, that such a distinguished officer could be a homosexual, and offend in such a frontal way against the purity of the master race. And so they sought to keep the whole affair hushed up in their own ranks, and brush it away in the individual cells of a concentration camp. The "lady's" face was very seldom seen, and that only at night. If he was allowed to go on living, and was not immediately liquidated, as the SS leadership would certainly have preferred, so as to remove any witness of this "scandal," the young man owed this to his father's influence with high-ups in the Nazi party, which certainly cost him a great deal of money.

I also learned from my Capo friend that the young man was very pretty, even for a girl, yet also had a good business sense. The Gypsy Capo must have known, for he made deals with this Hamburg businessman's son via the prisoners employed on domestic work in the bunker. In return for his jewelry, which was really valuable, and which he immediately broke up into its components, diamonds, pearls, and gold rings, he received substantial extra provisions, which were delivered to both him and the SS officer. I found that quite decent of the young man.

Thanks to this trade, these two prominent gays never had to suffer any real hunger, also because the young man's father immediately sent him a good deal of money. Yet they were not spared the pain of solitary confinement. When the camp was dissolved in 1945, the SS leadership wanted to have them shot, but in the general chaos they managed to escape in time in civilian clothes.

My Gypsy friend, however, made the deal of his life, and be came a rich man. Even if he exploited people in need such as these, he never cheated anyone. He remained, as I said, always true to his motto, "Live and let live," which made him a good business partner, fellow prisoner, and Capo.

6

COMMANDER "DUSTBAG"

IN MARCH 1941, the sadistic camp commander was dismissed and replaced. We men with the pink triangle had suffered very greatly under his rule, for he was always out to catch us in some infringement of regulations, with a view to ordering a beating on the "horse," which gave him such great pleasure. You can imagine what wishes of ours went with him on his departure.

When the new camp commander appeared, we homosexuals hoped very much that things would get at least somewhat better for us, and that the constant round of persecution and punishment would ease up a bit. Unfortunately it soon became clear that the new camp commander had even greater hatred and contempt for us gays than his predecessor.

He had the rank of an *SS Hauptsturmführer,* and had worked his way up from the ranks. How he ever became any kind of officer was a question that never ceased to amaze us, as he was quite lacking in any kind of culture. We later found out through the camp grapevine that before his career in the SS he had worked as a raftsman on the Bavarian rivers.

His first order was that our pink triangles should be replaced by new ones that were almost double in size. And over the triangle a yellow stripe should be sewn, 2 centimeters wide and 12 centimeters long.

"That's so I can recognize you filthy queer scum before you get close," he explained with a nasty smile. This first vexation was to prove not the only one. By a whole range of spiteful regulations, he managed to make the degrading and demeaning life of the concentration camp even harder for us, and drive several of us to an early grave. His special "hobby," however, as he called it, was dust. Time and again he would crawl into a dormitory in one block or another and look for dust—which naturally enough he always found. And when I say "crawl," I mean it quite literally. For this primitive creature in officer's uniform was quite lacking in shame, even before us prisoners, and really did crawl under the beds of us homosexuals, and of course always with success. Then he would scream at us, according with his level of culture: "You assholes, you butt-fuckers, you cocksuckers, I'll teach you a bit of tidiness, I'll make your asses boil." Then we would have to do fifty knee-bends and fifty sit-ups under his supervision, during which he would kick the weak prisoners in the rear so that they fell over, or shove his boots into their groins, while they were doing the sit-ups.

Because of these daily dust hunts, we came to call the commander "Dustbag." This nickname made the rounds of the whole camp, and even the SS block leaders and work detachment leaders came to use it among themselves. The commander soon got wind of the name, and flew into a rage, which gave both us prisoners and his SS underlings a good laugh. The nickname really stuck, for the whole time he remained in the camp.

But "Dustbag" also had other ways of cleaning up us queers. At night he would often slip into our dormitory to try and catch us *"in flagrante,"* in case any of us dared to try and make love. But since we had to have the light on all night long, he could never manage to sneak in unobserved, and so never caught anyone out in this way. In any case, nothing went on in our dormitory at night, given the electric lighting. Opportunities had to be found elsewhere. But "Dustbag's" failure to catch any of us out so enraged him that he was driven in his hatred to other measures against us.

Only four weeks after his appointment, he got the camp commandant to order that our dormitory A, the "queer" wing, was to be disbanded, and we were to be divided up among the other blocks in groups of thirty, with the exception of the Jewish blocks. Purely by accident I remained with twenty-six other people in my old dormitory, which was then filled up with "reds" and "greens"—that is, politicals and criminals. Now, we pink-triangle prisoners no longer had to keep our hands outside the blankets while we slept, and the lights were also switched off at night. At last we could get a better night's sleep, no longer disturbed by the light, given that we'd got used to the coughs and belches of two hundred other men in the room.

This new distribution, however, was not an arrangement that sprang from any human feeling on the part of our camp commander. Quite the contrary, he wanted to make us homosexuals feel safer in the other blocks and possibly get involved in sexual relations with other prisoners. He had spies in various dormitories, who would report any goings-on to him. "Dustbag" was out to get us one way or another.

Naturally enough, reports were made, and those accused were punished by twenty-five strokes on the "horse," which was already very severe, made worse by being given naked. "Dustbag" was in his element; once again he'd managed to give the "queers" what for.

I really wanted to get revenge on those spies and informers among the prisoners who had collaborated with the SS torturers, in some way or another. And I did everything against them that lay in my modest power. If I got to know one of the informers, and his name was confirmed by the man who'd been punished, then I pleaded with my Gypsy Capo until he arranged for the spy to be assigned an especially hard job within his work detachment, while he would also for weeks receive no extra rations, such as could be bought from the Capos on the black market, since his Capo would refuse to sell to him. Since all the "green" Capos stuck together, and many of them were in fact dependent on my Capo friend, the Gypsy was always able to grant my request.

Soon word got around that these spies got worse jobs shortly after informing to the SS, and suffered accordingly. "Dustbag," however, was quite unconcerned for his informants once a "queer" offender had been punished; that was all he cared about. And so after a few weeks the flow of information dried up, the collaborators having a deadly fear of even harder work and hunger. I am still proud today that I managed to carry out a personal justice and punishment on these spies.

A further new instruction from "Dustbag" shed yet more light on his character. When he spoke to a prisoner and asked for his name, the prisoner was not permitted to give his family name, but had to refer to himself simply as "Prisoner no. 4567," for example. If he asked one of us gays, however, then we were no longer to answer, "Sexual offender no. 4567," as with the previous camp commander, but had to say, "Queer asshole no. 4567." "Dustbag" would then give a brutal and cynical smile, for an answer like that fitted his own vocabulary and level of culture.

Through one of his spies among the prisoners he once learned that prisoners who worked in the kitchens were cooking privately at night and selling the food to the block seniors and Capos. The very same night he slunk into the kitchen and found a saucepan with more than thirty dumplings. He triumphantly reported this to the camp commandant, who appeared the next morning at roll call, and demanded an exemplary punishment for the kitchen staff and kitchen Capos. The commandant heard the report with a stem face, and told "Dustbag" he should produce the dumplings straightaway as evidence. "Dustbag" ran over to the kitchen block to fetch the saucepan. But when he burst into the kitchen, all he found in the pan were large round stones, about the size of the dumplings. He started cursing and swearing about the "gang of thieves," the "criminal rabble" who'd tricked him, and took the saucepan with the stones in it to the commandant, so that he could also see the scandalous abuse and trickery that had been perpetrated.

When the commandant saw the stones in the saucepan, he was convulsed with laughter, which made "Dustbag" fly into an even greater rage. The commandant then asked the kitchen Capo whether he had let any secret cooking of dumplings go on, which the Capo immediately denied with the straightest of faces. And when asked what the stones were doing in the saucepan, the Capo replied that they were used as bed warmers, since two of the kitchen staff had stomachaches. The commandant realized very well that the officer was the victim of a practical joke, but because he couldn't stand "Dustbag" for his low-class behavior, which had nothing officerlike about it, and in no way considered him as an equal, he was quite happy to leave him high and dry. He made his departure with the words: "Next time keep a careful check on the kitchen," and vanished with a grin.

It took a long while for "Dustbag" to forget this affront to his dignity. He came down hard on the "green" kitchen Capo, but he couldn't dismiss him, as he had been appointed by the commandant and seemed to have some credit with him.

Once I quite unintentionally crossed paths with "Dustbag" and almost collided with him. It was a Sunday, and I was on my way out of the dayroom to stretch my legs. He was just coming in, and as we were both moving rather quickly, I almost ran straight into him. He immediately started screaming that I had intentionally struck him. The block leader was called in and "Dustbag" condemned me to a half-hour's "tree hanging," with the block leader to execute the punishment.

"Tree hanging" was one of the most torturous punishments that could be inflicted. There was a strong, high pole, fitted into a specially placed hole in the ground, with a firm hook about two meters up. The victim had his hands tied behind his back, and was then strung up on the hook by his hands. The weight of the body then fell on the shoulders in such a way that you could keep yourself up for only a very short time. Very soon, your strength was exhausted and your shoulders were twisted round, which gave rise to terrible pains. No matter how hard you tried, you couldn't reach the ground with your toes. This punishment was thus particularly feared. When a prisoner was hanging from the "tree," his cries for help and screams of pain could be heard even from the other end of the camp.

Now I was myself to be punished in this way. The pole that belonged to our block was already placed in its hole, and my hands were tied behind my back. "Dustbag" gave an ugly smile and vanished in the direction of his office. Once again he had shown one of the queers how much he hated us and how fond he was of inflicting punishments on us. My block leader, for his part, took his time, while I was sweating all over with terror.

Suddenly my ex-lover, the camp senior, appeared and spoke quietly to the block leader. He looked at me for a few seconds, seeming slightly annoyed, and disappeared into the office. The senior cut through the rope, slapped me on the shoulders, and sent me off with the words: "Take care you don't fall into the hands of that asshole again, lad, you've got off okay this time." I pressed his hand in thanks and returned to the dayroom, still shaking and sweating in agitation, where I was congratulated by my fellow prisoners. Only then did I begin to relax. What the camp senior had said to the block leader I don't know, only that he had some power that he could occasionally use with certain SS men, so as to help prisoners and protect them from punishment—if he chose.

Shortly after this, my Gypsy Capo and his work detachment were sent to an outside camp at Würzburg. To give me some time to keep out of "Dustbag's" sight, the camp senior arranged that I should be taken along as well as clerk. The Gypsy's own wish to have me there with him must also have helped a lot.

We traveled to Würzburg in a truck, in the charge of an SS sergeant and six guards. There we were to construct a mineral bath for the SS in a hospital where the nurses were nuns. The twenty-five of us prisoners were billeted in the convent attached to the hospital, and also taken care of by the nuns.

On the very first day I had to prepare and clean the room where we were to sleep. There were no bunks or beds, but straw sacks arranged along the two longer sides of the room so as to leave a wide gangway free in the middle. Each of us received a thick blanket from the hospital stores. In one corner of the room I arranged space for myself and my Capo. When the sergeant came along in the evening to inspect the room, he asked me where I was going to sleep, and when I showed him the corner I had reserved, he cynically said: "And I suppose your friend the Gypsy Capo will be next to you." I admitted this, and looked at him quite innocently, but he only shook his head and said with a grin as he left: "Enjoy yourself, Donna Clara."

My Capo friend assigned me to the sisters as auxiliary, to help the nuns who cooked for us with the heavier tasks. I was also to keep our bedroom in order. The nuns were extremely nice and kind, even though the SS had warned them about us as dangerous criminals and subversives.

The sisters were very sympathetic when I told them about my home, as I was a Catholic and knew large sections of the liturgy by heart, remembering it from the time I served as an acolyte. I explained to them the different colored badges that the concentration-camp prisoners had, and how my pink triangle was the sign for homosexuals. I told the nuns about the brutalities of the SS, and about the many sufferings endured by the Jews, the politicals, and the Jehovah's Witnesses. I also mentioned the Gypsies, who were very strictly Catholic.

The sisters were incensed by my descriptions, and were at first unwilling to believe that such terrible and inhumane things could be done to the prisoners by the guards. This was the first time that they learned of the atrocities committed in the concentration camps, having no suspicion that the Hitler regime was ridding itself of its opponents and undesirables by torture and murder. My stories revealed to them an entire new world of evil.

When we returned to the convent for lunch on the first day of our work, the nuns showed us into a room apart, adjoining our sleeping quarters. When we unsuspectingly entered the room, we were struck dumb with surprise. Instead of our metal dishes, we found a long table covered with a white cloth, decked with porcelain dishes with floral pattern and gold surround, and shining silver cutlery. There were crystal vases filled with flowers, and burning candles gave quite a festive atmosphere. It was like a wedding feast in a palace.

We sat down at the table and ate our soup, tears running down our cheeks. All of us felt homesick for the civilized customs we had left behind. After years of vegetating in the Nazi camps, we were sitting down once again, for the first time, to a holiday meal. Many of us, perhaps, had never eaten at such a fine table, and their joy was doubled.

After the soup we had meat loaf with roast potatoes and gravy, washed down with cider. We were overcome by the feast, and as happy as children. Not an angry word was spoken, as was so often in our concentration-camp meal breaks, and everyone tried to accept the gift in the best spirit possible, with thankful glances and appreciative comments for the nuns who served us.

Our SS sergeant and his men, meanwhile, were seated in another room, at an equally fine table to our own. They were unaware, however, that their prisoners were being treated the same. We were still in the middle of eating when the sergeant walked into our room and was most astonished and put out to see our arrangements. In angry tones he instructed the nuns never to do this again. We prisoners had to eat out of our metal bowls, and must not sit at a table like this; after all we were a band of criminals, and not visiting monks. The nuns had not expected the sergeant to protest so vigorously, and promised to serve our meals in future in the manner laid down. In order to spare us prisoners any reprisals from the SS, they carried out his instructions. We had again to eat out of metal dishes, though we could at least sit at a proper table. But we could never forget the holiday banquet the nuns had given us. Not only did we speak of it for months after, but the story even made the rounds in other camps.

On the fourth day of our stay in Würzburg the SS sergeant relieved me of my job as auxiliary to the nuns, fearing I would tell them about the concentration camp and give them an insight into the conditions there. He didn't know that the nuns were already well informed about the brutalities and murderous practices of the SS.

I had to join other prisoners in their outdoor work, but as arranged, I only helped my Capo with the clerical tasks. My work in Würzburg was not strenuous, and even the other prisoners had nothing to suffer there, for the SS guards fore-bore from any brutalities or excesses on account of the observant eyes of the nuns. We got plenty to eat, and the nuns even smuggled us cigarettes. They were cunning enough, however, to provide the SS guards and their sergeant with everything they might want, so that they felt well looked after and left us in peace. I therefore had a few relatively peaceful days with my Gypsy Capo, and even some relatively peaceful nights.

After three weeks, however, I was sent back to Flossenbürg to continue work in the building material stores. The Capo in charge had got me called back, ostensibly because my replacement had made too many mistakes and the records had fallen into disorder. The truth, however, was that he was keen on me. He was one of the two Capos whom my Gypsy friend had paid off so that they would leave me to him. But now that my Gypsy Capo was away for a good while, it seemed a good opportunity for the building stores Capo to call me back as an indispensable clerk and get together with me without the Gypsy interfering—that is, if I was willing.

And because hunger is painful, and I had got used to having enough to eat, thanks to my Gypsy Capo and my previous Capo friend, and also because I still had to fear losing my cushy position, I had no choice but to accept.

One thing was, of course, quite clear to me: my will to survive the concentration camp was uncommonly strong, but any such survival against the brutes of the SS had a high price, the price of morality, decency, and honor. I knew this and suffered on account of it, yet without such friendships with Capos I should not be alive today. *C'est la vie!* Sarcastically, I turned my Gypsy friend's motto "Live and let live" into my own motto: "Live and let love."

My Gypsy friend returned a few weeks later, but with serious injuries to his face, hands, and chest. He was taken to the Flossenbürg sick bay. He hadn't taken cover sufficiently quickly in Würzburg when some dynamiting was being done, or else the charge had gone off prematurely. Naturally the news spread like wildfire among the Capos, and it was already said that there would be a sure struggle between him and the building stores Capo when the Gypsy Capo recovered—a struggle over me. I rightly feared that I would be ground between two stones, in a way that could cost me my life.

I accordingly placed myself fair and square behind my new friend, and told him this quite openly. All I asked of him was that he should let me go and visit the Gypsy in the sick bay, for I was indebted to him for his many presents and favors. But the Capos and seniors didn't want to allow this, fearing that the love between him and me could flare up again, and that the homosexual relationships of other "dignitaries" would be endangered by an SS investigation, something that would create chaos and dismissals all round, not to mention punishments. For the politicals, however, this was a golden opportunity, as they thought they could boot out the "greens" and seize power for themselves. I naturally understood these objections and considerations on the part of the "dignitaries," but I refused to let them prevail over me, and begged and pleaded until the camp senior, who still had a strong platonic feeling for me, decided that I could visit the Gypsy in the white clothing of a nurse, with a red-cross armband. He let the Capo in the sick bay in on this, so that everything would go off without accident. I softly entered the sickroom, while the medical Capo stood guard, to warn me in case an SS man should unexpectedly appear. Cautiously I approached the Gypsy Capo's bed. His hands, chest, and head were completely swathed in bandages, only his eyes and mouth left free. His eyes were still closed when I spoke gently to him and said: "Hello, Stefan. Can you hear me? I'm so worried about you." Then he opened his eyes, which shone with joy at seeing me again. He couldn't speak, but my surprise visit touched him so much that it brought tears to his eyes. I wanted to touch him even though his hands and body were covered, so I pressed his knees and rested my hand on his leg. He gazed at me tearfully, while I sat with him a good five minutes. He certainly wanted to tell me something, but he couldn't even move his head, let alone speak. As I left, I kissed his bandaged forehead. "I can't stay longer, I only want to tell you that we'll get you well again. The seniors intend to get you out alive. Good-bye, Stefan, get well soon, and thank you for everything."

And indeed, he was taken care of and recovered. He was a favorite and trusted lieutenant of the camp senior, and as soon as he could leave his sickbed he had him sent back again to Würzburg in charge of the work detachment there, wishing to avoid any dispute between the Gypsy and my new Capo friend, who was also a favorite of his. Without seeing me again, he was suddenly whisked off.

I had particular admiration for the camp senior on this occasion, for arranging everything for the best and managing things with the SS officers. "Well, it only takes a few presents to buy friendship," the senior said, and that applied even to the SS in Flossenbürg concentration camp.

The Gypsy Capo remained in Würzburg for almost a year. When he returned to Flossenbürg with his detachment, a genuine brothel for prisoners was established in the camp by the SS, as I shall go on to relate. The Gypsy Capo, moreover, now found among the girls forcibly inducted there a Gypsy girl whom he regularly visited. From then on he was no longer actively homosexual, though he still remained very friendly to me, and whenever he saw me alone, he would squeeze my behind and say in his thick Hungarian accent: "You crazy boy, you!"

7

BURNINGS AND TORTURES

ON HOME-BUILT RADIOS, mostly constructed and operated by the politicals, the camp seniors and a section of the prisoners who were known as reliable opponents of the Nazis learned not only about the political situation within the Reich, but also what was being said abroad about Nazi Germany. So we did not just find out about the invasion of Russia from the official camp radio, being forced to listen to Hitler's broadcast speeches on the parade ground, we also learned of the resistance by Germany's enemies on our own secret radios.

Thanks to the political activity of the red-triangle prisoners, we were better informed of the real war situation than were the German people at large.

One day in late July 1941, the command came over the loudspeaker that all prisoners had immediately to return to their dormitories and sit there on the ground. No one must look out of the window, and anyone caught doing so by the guards would be shot without warning. We sat on the floor of our dayroom for more than an hour, until we finally heard the command to go back to work.

The whole camp was naturally like a swarm of frightened bees, even if we all acted in front of the SS as if we had no interest in finding out why we had to return to our quarters and could not look out of the window. Among ourselves, however, we passed messages of encouragement, and most people concluded that perhaps some of the Nazi leaders had turned against Hitler and been secretly put in the camp.

We rapidly learned the truth. More than a hundred Russian officers had been secretly brought to Flossenbürg. By the red braid on their caps we took them for political commissars, a suspicion that was later confirmed. It was still unclear, however, why they had been brought so secretly to the concentration camp. The very next day, however, we found this out, for in the morning we heard long drawn-out rifle fire coming from the corner of the camp, where prisoners sentenced to death were customarily shot. This was obviously what was going on now, too. In fact, all Russian political commissars were shot by the SS, if they refused to betray their country.

Since the shooting ground was completely covered with concrete, hundreds of liters of blood from the dead Russians flowed through a drain into a little stream, which for hours became a literal river of blood. Not far from the Flossenbürg railway station there was a large pond, which this stream flowed into, and at the far end also flowed out. After this first mass shooting, the water was red only at the pond inlet, but after the third shooting of Russian officers, ten days later, the whole pond was colored with the blood of the victims, and terrible to see. Everyone in the camp knew this from the work detachment that had been in the vicinity and told us about it.

The civilian population, through their mayor, complained to the SS commandant about the pollution of their pond, also to the local party leadership, and demanded an immediate halt to the inflow of blood. The village inhabitants were already familiar enough with the brutalities that the SS practiced on the prisoners, having seen these at the worksites outside the camp, and quite well acquainted too, undoubtedly, with the tortures committed inside, but their blood red pond was a bit much even for them.

The shootings behind the crematorium were now suspended, in order to pacify the local population, but the killings continued, in great majority Russian commissars, officers, and soldiers, simply with other methods being used.

In place of the SS firing squads, the SS camp doctor and his aides now carried out the murders. These took place in the same building where the crematorium was housed. The prisoner entered a waiting room, where he had to strip completely—for a medical examination, he was told—and then into the doctor's "surgery," as called in by a nurse. There an aide who spoke Russian, in fact a prisoner, told him he was going to receive an injection against cholera and dysentery. In fact, the doctor injected the victim with hydrogen, which brought on sudden death.

At the other end the doctor's room had a second door leading out onto a hall, where the murdered Russian officers were laid out in rows, on top of one another, until they were burnt. I will say more about these mass cremations later. The Russian officers' uniforms were carefully sorted by prisoners, and when banknotes, papers, and objects of value had been extracted, they were taken to a special store. Later on, these uniforms, together with the papers and personal effects, were sent to the Dirlewanger SS division, and partly also to the Wehrmacht. They were presumably worn by German agents and sabotage forces who operated behind the Russian frontline.

When the flow of prisoners for liquidation persisted, and a transport of some twenty to thirty men generally arrived in Flossenbürg at least twice a week, we were no longer sent back to our blocks, but could carry on our usual work. The SS no longer needed to conceal what was going on, since everyone in the camp knew about the mass murders. We could generally tell immediately precisely what group were being taken to be murdered in the crematorium building. They were not always Russian officers and soldiers, but also civilians from Poland, Ukraine, and White Russia.

The camp doctor, however, who showed little humanity in dealing with us prisoners, and was now giving these mass "injections" in the crematorium, must suddenly have remembered his Hippocratic oath, which required that he should heal the sick and not murder people who were well, for he refused to give any more injections. Even though he had been so keen on "research and experiment" on living prisoners, who subsequently died, he was now stricken with pangs of conscience. This didn't make him any better or more humane. For both as doctor and as human being he should have refused to give the very first injection. He obtained special leave and was subsequently sent to the front at his own request. His prisoner-assistant who had served as interpreter for the Russians turned round and hanged himself, at about the same time as the doctor departed—a further victim of the mass murders. He had often asked to be relieved of his duty, but the only answer he ever got was a beating.

The new camp doctor, a fanatical SS man who seemed quite ignorant of any human ethic, let alone medical, immediately introduced economy measures. In order to save on hydrogen, he gave the victims injections of air, which similarly led to their immediate death. In this way he carried on with good conscience what had proved too much for his predecessor. Anyone who entered the crematorium building came out only as a corpse.

Since this crematorium was too small to incinerate so many bodies, an open incinerator was built just behind the crematorium, to dispense as rapidly as possible with the mass injection victims. The large number of prisoners who perished in the camp were also brought here.

The corpses were stacked in layers between thick pieces of wood, then gasoline was poured over and set alight by a long stick with a bundle of rags on the end. The prisoners who had to do this work were given an ample ration of alcohol, to enable them to cope with the penetrating stench and thick smoke, and were generally blind drunk. These prisoners were themselves liquidated by the SS later on, so that they could not tell other people of the mass slaughter and incineration of these Russians and Poles.

It often happened that some "corpses" would start to crawl out when the pyre was set alight. The injection hadn't killed them but only made them faint, and they had just been thrown in together with other corpses. Whether the drink-sozzled prisoners were aware of this or not we shall never know. The rapid rise in temperature brought the victims round, and they scrambled out of the flames with singed hair and skin, generally crawling on all fours and already with severe burns on their bodies. Very few of them could scream; they were so overcome by shock and terror that they simply whimpered and rattled, their eyes and mouths gaping wide.

If they managed to crawl out of the burning fire, these half-dead naked men, still numbed by the injections, had to be shoved back into the flames with long sticks by the drunken prisoners who worked there, perhaps more than once, until they finally disappeared in the smoke and flames.

And all this happened on the order and under the supervision of the SS, that select crop of the German Reich, the "people of poets and thinkers."

In autumn 1941 the Flossenbürg building division was assigned a new SS sergeant, sent here from another concentration camp. The building material stores where I was employed was also put under his command. All the Capos and prisoners working under him had to appear for inspection, and he went through our ranks in turn.

First of all he asked each Capo for his name, origin, and profession, then had them step to one side. Now it was the turn of us "ordinary" prisoners. Some of us wore the pink triangle, and when we came up before the sergeant, the first thing he did was to spit at each of us in the face, to show his profound contempt for homosexuals in the most forceful manner. Any one of us who didn't stand up straight enough, or answer sufficiently quickly, he hit across the face with his stick, so hard that the victim generally fell to the floor, with two or three teeth broken.

As clerk, I came last in the line, so it is easy to imagine my increasing fear as my turn with the beast approached. When he finally got to me, he saw my pink triangle and spat at me right on the mouth.

"Where do you come from, you filthy queer?"

"From Vienna, *Herr Hauptscharführer.*"

"And where's that dump then?"

What a cretin, I thought, and answered immediately: "In Austria, *Herr Hauptscharführer.*"

"What's that, you swine? Austria? It's called Ostmark, you lump of shit. So you're not only a queer, you're a Communist as well!" he screamed, cursing me and beating me until I collapsed.

I'd really had it now. In my anxiety not to make any mistake, I'd been overhasty and said "Osterreich" instead of "Ostmark," as Hitler had rebaptized my native country. I got several kicks as well for this, as I lay on the ground.

I was reported and sentenced to three days' arrest in the bunker, without bread or water, and in darkness. Fortunately, when I was received in the bunker by the Capo in charge, he had already been bribed by my Capo friend. Although I was put in a single cell, it was not a darkened one. A prisoner medic, moreover, came over from the sick bay and treated me, again of course at the instigation of my Capo and thanks to his payment. I also got food and water, though I was strictly guarded by the Capo in charge of the bunker, so that no SS man, not even the sentry in charge of the bunker, came to check on me.

Once again I owed my good fortune to my friendship with a Capo, coming through this incident unscathed and being spared many tortures. For all the "green" Capos stuck together and were always prepared to help one another out. Even though the bunker Capo was a vicious sadist, he looked after me like a soft-boiled egg in order to oblige his Capo colleague, especially as this request was backed up with hard cash.

What I saw and heard in the bunker, in those three days, surpassed even the brutalities and tortures I had witnessed so far. My cell was not in fact designed as a prison punishment cell, but simply used as a storeroom, so that it was scarcely noticed or checked by the SS sergeant in charge of the bunker. That was why I had been put in there by the bunker Capo. Since the sergeant in charge was very lax, and left the prisoners' records to his Capo to deal with, the Capo could keep my presence from the knowledge of his boss. My cell door had some thin cracks in it, through which it was possible to see very well and observe the main corridor. It was in this corridor, as I soon learned, that the torture of prisoners sent to the bunker took place.

While I was there, a prisoner with a pink triangle, from Innsbruck in Austria, was tortured to death in the bunker. He was stripped naked and his hands tied to a hook in the wall so that his body hung in the air, and he couldn't touch the ground with his feet. Two or three SS men who were assigned to the cell block, as the bunker was officially known, stood around and waited for the "performance" to start—that is, the torture of the Tirol lad.

The first "game" that the SS sergeant and his men played was to tickle their victim with goose feathers, on the soles of his feet, between his legs, in the armpits, and on other parts of his naked body. At first the prisoner forced himself to keep silent, while his eyes twitched in fear and torment from one SS man to the other. Then he could not restrain himself and finally he broke out in a high-pitched laughter that very soon turned into a cry of pain, while the tears ran down his face, and his body twisted against his chains. After this tickling torture, they let the lad hang there for a little, while a flood of tears ran down his cheeks and he cried and sobbed uncontrollably.

But the depraved SS men were set on having a lot more fun with this poor creature. The bunker Capo had to bring two metal bowls, one filled with cold water and the other with hot. "Now we're going to boil your eggs for you, you filthy queer, you'll soon feel warm enough,"[1] the bunker officer said gleefully, raising the bowl with hot water between the victim's thighs so that his balls hung down into it. The prisoner let out a shattering scream for help, the pain hurt him so much. He tried to struggle free or roll to one side, but the ties on his hands and feet held him tight.

"Give him the cold water, then, he's already hot, the filthy swine," one of the SS men laughed brutally, whereupon the SS butchers took up the cold water and placed this bowl between their victim's thighs. Again he screamed in agony, for the cold water must have been excruciating after the extreme heat. Time and again he tried to break free from his chains, but he just exhausted himself fruitlessly.

This procedure was repeated several times, until the tormented victim lost consciousness, after he had screamed him-

---

1   Another pun on *"warmer Bruder";* see p. 35.

self hoarse and could now only emit a kind of gurgle. A bucket of cold water was thrown over him to bring him round, then the torture was started again, with bits of skin now hanging visibly down from the victim's scalded scrotum.

While carrying out these tortures, the SS monsters got through a bottle or two of spirits that they passed round. They were already quite drunk when they hit upon a new torture that could only have been thought up in the brain of someone totally perverted.

"He's a butt-fucker, isn't he, let him have what he wants," growled one of the SS men, taking up a broom that stood in the comer and shoving the handle deep into the prisoner's anus. He was already incapable of screaming anymore—his voice had simply seized up with pain—but his body jerked and tore at the chains; there was still a lot of life left in the lad. But the SS men only laughed the louder at the "filthy queer," who moved his lips as if to cry out without any sound emerging.

Finally they cut the fainting man down and let him fall to the floor, where he lay in a heap without stirring, his limbs bent under him. The drunken SS men staggered out into the open, but the last of them stumbled over the martyred prisoner who was still lying on the ground. Angrily he kicked the victim with the toe of his boot, and he began to stir again.

"The filthy queer's still alive," he burbled, taking up a wooden stool that was standing next to the wall and bringing it down with all his force on the victim's head. This finally freed the poor martyr from his pains, for now he was really dead.

While I was watching this torture of my fellow victim, I had to put my fingers in my mouth and bite on them constantly, to keep from screaming out in rage. But when the boy was struck with the wooden stool I could no longer control myself and cried out: "Beasts! You beasts!" The drunken murderers, however, didn't hear; they had already left.

The bunker Capo burst into my cell and raised his hand imploringly. "You stupid idiot, shut your mouth, or do you want to be killed as well?" He seized onto my jacket and flung me back and forward to shake me out of my hysteria. A liberating flood of tears suddenly broke from my eyes, over the terrible and tormented death of my Austrian countryman.

I was very glad indeed on the third day when the camp senior personally came to fetch me from the bunker, for the death of the Tirol lad had thrown me into a deep depression, and I kept breaking into more fits of sobbing.

"Don't make such a scene, lad, quiet down. Believe me, the day is coming when everything that's been done to us will be repaid. And as far as the new SS asshole in your department goes, let me deal with him, he'll soon go the way of the others."

With a friendly pat on my bottom, he went away.

Christmas came around, the time for remembering our families. Not that we prisoners were left much time—our SS guards took good care of that. But in externals, at least, they acted as if Christmas was a festival of joy even for us. Fourteen days before Christmas Eve, a tree more than 10 meters tall was already erected on the parade ground, and covered with electric lights. These were switched on as soon as it got dark, and the tree looked quite festive, even here. Naturally enough, talk among the prisoners centered on one theme alone, especially in the evenings: our families—wives, children, parents—as each of us yearned for home.

On the night of December 23–24, 1941, some Russian prisoners tried to break out of the camp, but were captured by the SS guards. Some of the Russians were shot immediately, the rest, eight men, hanged on the morning of the twenty-fourth.

In order to humiliate those of us who were Christians, and presumably as a "sacrifice" to their "Germanic god," the death sentence was carried out beside the Christmas tree, to the left and right of which long horizontal posts were erected on wooden supports, with four victims being tied up and hanged on either side. As a deterrent to any further escape attempt, or possibly to enhance the Christmas for us prisoners, the hanged men's corpses were left in place for more than two days, until the Christmas feast was over.

A still meaner trick was the order of the camp commander that on Christmas Eve itself, two blocks had to appear in full strength in front of the Christmas tree and sing carols for a good half hour. A gruesome picture of a grotesque situation. While the crackling male chorus sang: "O Christmas tree, o Christmas tree, how green are your branches . . . ," the eight dead soldiers hung from their gallows and were swung to and fro by the wind.

I have never been able to rid myself of this terrible sight, and every Christmas, whenever I hear a carol sung—no matter how beautifully—I remember the Christmas tree at Flossenbürg with its grisly "decorations."

8

A PINK-TRIANGLED CAPO

EARLY IN 1942 the granite quarrying was suspended and work was transferred to aircraft production. Hitler needed every German male as a soldier in the occupied territories, so now we concentration-camp prisoners had to make munitions, in order that the workers formerly employed in this could be inducted into the German army. A plant for the Messerschmitt works was set up in our concentration camp, to make wings and tails for the various types of Messerschmitt planes. They were built in the long galleries that had been cut away into the quarry. The finished components were then transported by train and assembled somewhere else, we didn't know whether in another concentration camp or in one of the Messerschmitt factories proper.

Only the concentration-camp prisoners worked in the Flossenbürg factory, but we were taught the work by German civilian workers and staff, who continued to supervise our work from the technical aspect. These civilians were selected Nazi party members, and blindly loyal to the Hitler regime. At first they were aloof and contemptuous, and saw us only as slaves and criminals. But after the great defeat at Stalingrad had heralded the collapse of the German war machine, they became increasingly friendly, and often tried to make human contact with us, bringing us cigarettes and alcohol, most likely as a kind of insurance, for defeat became ever more likely each day.

The Flossenbürg camp, which was originally built to house 3,000 prisoners, had already been expanded several times in the course of the years, and in 1942 it had more than 10,000 prisoners, rising in 1943 to some 18,000. Since it was impossible to build new blocks fast enough, all the blocks were filled to overflowing. Instead of 150 men, each block housed up to 400, sometimes even more.

The majority of the inmates were now prisoners of war, or else foreigners from the occupied territories—mainly Russians and Poles, but also French, Dutch, and British, as well as Serbs, Hungarians, and Romanians.

If these foreigners were to work in the aircraft factory, German-speaking prisoners were also needed, for now work went on day and night, and in smaller groups than before, which meant that the demand for foremen and assistant foremen from the ranks of German prisoners grew ever greater. We "queers," too, were now brought in as assistant foremen, and, despite being "degenerates from the German nation," we now had the "great honor" of being permitted to work on arms production and so help lengthen the war. The SS leadership now discovered that we prisoners from the Reich were Germans after all.

In a fit of generosity, we were promised that we would all be released after the victorious end of the war, as long as we satisfactorily fulfilled our work in the aircraft factory. Even us German prisoners must ultimately feel ourselves to be Germans, and should serve our fatherland at the posts we were assigned. We, too, should do everything possible to contribute to the German victory and preserve the Third Reich. A fine speech from "Dustbag," this one, even if a vicious circle in its argument, though I wisely refrained from comment.

We German prisoners could now let our hair grow, of course only in the appropriate military style, but even so it made us look that much more human. A special order also came down from *SS Reichsführer* Himmler, that German prisoners should no longer be given corporal punishment without permission of the SS headquarters in Berlin. None of the camp commanders stuck to this order, and beatings continued, yet no longer so openly in front of other prisoners. All these favors bestowed on the German prisoners, however, did not apply to German Jews, let alone the Jews from the occupied territories. And as far as we were concerned, the pink-triangle prisoners, besides being allowed to let our hair grow we received hardly any other favors, and were still equated with the Jews in our treatment by the SS. We were still treated by our fellow prisoners, too, with contempt, as queers and "degenerates," still the human refuse that anyone could insult and tread upon.

Thanks to my good relationship with the camp senior and certain Capos, I became the first and only prisoner with the pink triangle to become a Capo and foreman in the aircraft factory. My former activity as clerk in the building material stores was also decisive for this, as I now became responsible for the stores in the factory. I had charge of the inventory and supply of parts and material needed to make the aircraft components, as well as of ordering further material from the Messerschmitt head office. This job was called the "station" detachment, since the stores were located right beside Flossenbürg railway station—that is, outside the camp perimeter. Naturally enough, I was placed under some civilians, who gave me instructions and passed on my orders for material to the head office. Later on, however, when everything went smoothly thanks to my organizational methods, the civilians simply said good morning, left me in charge of everything, and merely made spot checks.

The SS work detachment leader in charge of me also bothered himself little with my work, and confined himself to fetching our group from the camp in the morning and returning us there at night. He generally spent the day playing dice with the civilians, and otherwise enjoying himself. This station detachment, therefore, was not just an easy position for us prisoners, but also for the SS, and the civilians in the works as well.

My work detachment, whom I had charge of as Capo and foreman, was more than twenty-five strong. Apart from three German prisoners, two other homosexuals and a Jehovah's Witness, who served as assistant foremen, I had only Russians and Poles, who were civilians rather than prisoners of war. Since neither I nor the other three Germans could speak either Russian or Polish, any communication with our fellow workers was almost impossible, since they dourly answered every instruction with "Don't understand." At the start of our work in the stores, therefore, the assistant foremen had to locate all the components needed themselves, and simply give the parts to the Russians and Poles to pack up. When the boxes were filled, they were taken by another work detachment to the assembly shops in the quarry. This operation naturally led to serious delays in supplying the orders for parts, which we received every morning from the various assembly departments. To all intents it was only the three Germans who did the work, while the other prisoners, Russians and Poles, stood around with their hands in their pockets and just watched us.

I didn't like this at all, for quite apart from the injustice of such a division of labor within my group, I was afraid of being dismissed from my position of Capo for incompetence. As the only Capo with the pink triangle, I was already a thorn in the side of "Dustbag." There could be no persistent delays in the supply of materials, or else I'd get it in the neck for sabotage.

I had to think up some idea, and sifted the whole question through in my mind. In the end I hit on a simple solution, and gave all the parts a number. Naturally, each already had a long number given it by Messerschmitt themselves, but on top of this I gave the parts with which we dealt a simple number of my own. The official number might be 711 F 453457, but I would call it number 16. My number was larger and written in red, so as to be more prominent than the factory number.

Since the Russians and Poles either couldn't or wouldn't read German, they had previously been unable to collect parts by their factory numbers. In my new system, each of them received from the assistant foremen a list with my part numbers, and on receipt of an order the assistants had only to ask for the parts by the numbers I gave them.

Now that the Russian and Polish prisoners in my team were able to fulfil the orders for parts given them, they always did so correctly, so that there was no longer any delay.

The civilian workers and staff were extremely pleased by my innovation, especially when I explained to them that it would make any form of espionage significantly more difficult. They immediately reported this to their headquarters in Berlin, as well as to the SS office responsible for arms production in the concentration camps, so that my system of numbering could possibly be introduced in other concentration-camp factories where foreign prisoners were working. This made me an almost indispensable figure, and later on turned out to protect me from being sent to the front in a punishment company.

Of course I could not myself choose the prisoners who were assigned to my work team. Each team was at that time assigned from the camp office, and confirmed by the SS officer in charge, who held the high rank of a *Sturmbann-führer*. Since my "station" detachment lay far afield, outside the camp perimeter and surrounded by the civilian population, it was not subject to special checks from the SS guards, particularly from certain NCOs who liked to play the savage. I soon had the reputation of a gentle and reliable Capo, who was very energetic but never screamed at the prisoners, let alone struck any of them. My image as a "sticker" had already been well established in the ranks of the camp "dignitaries," from the descriptions of the camp senior at the time of our intimate acquaintance.

For these reasons, the block seniors and Capos requested the head Capo and camp senior to assign their young Poles and Russians—that is, their bed partners—to my work team, which they called "the sanatorium." For although the SS authorities certainly had a general idea of these homosexual relationships, any particular relationship that came to light was vigorously prosecuted and punished. Officially, therefore, the SS did not know that the young Poles and Russians assigned to the block seniors and Capos as servants also shared their beds. And since the "dignitaries" didn't want to run any risks, they managed to assign their young dolly-boys to my team, knowing that this would be a safe place for them.

None of these boys, who were generally between sixteen and twenty, was directly forced to take a position as "cleaner" with a Capo or block senior. But since they were always hungry, they themselves sought out such positions, and were very pleased to obtain them. Not surprising, for this brought more to eat and easier work, and the return service—that is, their boss's bed—very few of them, if any, found at all repugnant. There were often fights between them, if one of the boys tried to seduce the other's "boss," which they might do for instance if he was known to be particularly generous. I treated them with great understanding, for until my appointment as Capo I had myself been in the same position, from the same need for good food and easy work.

It turned out, therefore, that out of twenty-five or so men in my team, some eighteen to twenty were always these dolly-boys. It was not hard to tell them from the mass of other prisoners in the camp, as they looked almost well fed and almost always wore well-fitting and clean prison clothing. At first, they thought themselves somewhat above other people, and hoped that my goodwill toward them meant they could escape work altogether. They wanted just to stand around in the stores and watch the others working, or sit in a corner and play cards. Since I never followed up my warnings with blows, they took this as a weakness, and thought they could do what they liked.

On the second evening, however, I went to see the camp senior and complained about these boys, who countered every instruction from me with the words: "My boss says I no work." I brought his attention to the danger that the other prisoners in my team could complain about the situation to the NCO in charge, which might mean the sexual relationships between the boys and the Capos becoming known to the SS. This was an alarm signal for the camp senior, and he thanked me for coming to him immediately and telling him the problem.

"I'll soon give these fat layabouts what for," he said, and immediately called all the block seniors and Capos who had boys in my team to his office. In my presence, he brought home to them in no uncertain terms that their bed partners had to work and must unconditionally obey my instructions, if they wanted to avoid complaints from the rest of my team and the consequent loss of their dolly-boys.

"Okay, then, lads, you tell your boys this, and give them a good tanning so that they know what's the matter. Otherwise they'll put us all in danger and our position in the camp. Go back to your boys and knock some sense into them. Box their ears first, make love afterward," he joked, and the others had a good laugh with him.

Ever since then, the young Poles and Russians worked the same as the other prisoners. The day after my interview with the camp senior they swore a lot in their own languages, and though I couldn't understand, I could see from their expressions that their "bosses" had given them all a sound thrashing, as the camp senior had ordered, though that they didn't know. What surprised them was how they had all got similar treatment the same evening. But they were happy to have a good laugh about it. From now on, moreover, they did everything I said without trouble, and obligingly carried out all my instructions. "You good comrade, don't hit, don't swear, always good," they often said to me, and I was indeed less like a Capo to them than an elder comrade.

Work in my "station" detachment, moreover, was anything but hard, and really was like a rest cure, a "sanatorium," for prisoners working under me. It only took a few hours to make up the orders for parts and dispatch them in their containers. Then we could chat and have a smoke, if anyone had any tobacco, or else play cards. One of the prisoners would stand guard at the window, relieved every hour, and warn us of the approach of an SS man or civilian employee. When this happened, everyone would take up some component or other and go busily round the shelves until the checkup had finished and we were left in peace. I would report smartly not only to any SS guard who came to check up on the stores, but also to the civilians, which never failed to make an impression. Since everything in my department seemed right and proper, and supplies were sent off in good time, these checks were kept to at most one or two visits per day, which gave us a lot of time to ourselves.

One particular advantage from my Capo position was that all the block seniors and Capos who had their dolly-boys in my department would be very willing to do favors for me and supplied me with nice bits of food and tobacco, even giving me money on occasion. Since I was now a Capo myself, I took leave of my former Capo friend from the building division. First of all, any sexual relation between Capos was unthinkable and would not be tolerated by the "dignitaries," while secondly, I no longer needed a relationship of convenience such as this for the sake of mere survival. I was now a "dignitary" myself, which gave me a certain position of power in the camp—not one I could exercise directly for myself, but one that the other "dignitaries" who had their boys in my work detachment had need of.

Since I now had enough to eat, I got into a relationship with another German pink-triangle prisoner—no relationship of convenience this time, but a genuine one, based on mutual understanding and trust. We got on very well together, and were as happy as anyone could be said to be in concentration camp. On my instigation, of course, he was assigned to my unit as assistant foreman, which was not so easy and cost a heavy bribe.

My new friend was from Magdeburg, aged twenty-six, and had served in the navy until caught by the military police in a toilet with another young serviceman, while he was home on leave. After serving a six-month sentence in the Torgau military prison he was sent to Flossenbürg, for some inexplicable reason, instead of the more usual course of a punishment company at the front. Here he survived, thanks to the assistance that I managed to mobilize, until the camp was dissolved in 1945, even though he was often threatened with being sent to the Dirlewanger penal division commanded by the SS.

When our work detachment returned to camp in the evening, we had always to wait at the camp gate until we'd been counted. Whether the returning prisoners were alive or dead was a matter of indifference to the SS; all that was important was the number.

One evening, "Dustbag" stood at the gate and watched the various outside work detachments returning. When I approached with my troop, marching in fives, I could already see him standing at the camp gate, seemingly in wait for us. I halted my group smartly in front of the gate, and reported: "Station detachment with one Capo and twenty-seven men, returning from work duty."

"Dustbag" gave me an ugly smile and stroked my pink triangle with his stick. "A very pale red, that one. Or is it really pink? What, a queer as Capo, that's something we haven't seen before."

He dug his stick forcefully into my stomach. I stood still, and waited for his command to enter.

But "Dustbag" still wanted his bit of fun. He examined the rows of prisoners in my detachment, and said with a cynical grin: "You've got some well-fed-looking lads there. What's this, then, a scout troop? But we won't have any scouting here, I don't think . . ." Then he went from one of the lads to the next, lifting up the tails of their jackets with his stick and commenting: "Who does this nice bit of ass belong to, then, your Capo I suppose?"

The young Russians and Poles just shook their heads in denial, but this only made "Dustbag" more angry, as he was sure I must have a relationship with one of them. He didn't know that they'd been put into my detachment by their block seniors and Capos, and that it was these whom they had relationships with. He was almost sure that I worked my way through each of them in turn.

The SS men who were standing around were creased up with laughter, as most of them knew very well who slept with whom. But this laughter enraged "Dustbag" all the more, and he angrily gave the instruction that from then on, when I went through the gate with my unit, I should no longer announce myself with the words: "Station detachment," but say instead: "Butt-fuckers' detachment."

This went on for a few days, giving the SS guards a good laugh each time that I had to announce myself in this way. Several of the SS men added to the joke by calling, "Have a good time," or something similar after us.

One day, however, the commandant was at the gate to watch the prisoners coming in. He'll be surprised by the odd name of my work detachment, I thought to myself, and announced in a particularly loud voice: "Butt-fuckers' detachment with one Capo and twenty-seven men returning from work!" so that he couldn't help but hear. He immediately came up to me and angrily asked, "What kind of a report is that? Who told you to say that? I'm not having any more of that rubbish, do you understand?"

"Yes, *Herr Kommandant.*"

He insisted on knowing who had ordered me to report in this way, but I kept obstinately silent and simply shrugged my shoulders, not wanting to bring down on myself "Dustbag's" revenge for this "betrayal." The commandant, however, read my silence very well, and ordered the SS sergeant in charge of our detachment to tell him, he being only too glad to name "Dustbag" as the instigator. The commandant expressly ordered me once again to report in future only with the correct title of my detachment, and went off shaking his head.

The very next day, "Dustbag" was again at the gate, looking particularly annoyed. I was sure that the commandant had had a word with him. I smartly reported the arrival of "station detachment," and he immediately asked me: "Was it you who betrayed me to the commandant, you swine?" "No,

Herr Lagerführer, I didn't say anything, it was the *Herr Ober-scharführer* who had to tell the *Herr Lagerkommandant*."

"Dustbag" looked at me in disbelief, and turned to the sergeant, but he simply confirmed what I'd said. "Dustbag" turned away, saying: "I wouldn't have suspected such strength of character in a filthy queer," and ordered us in.

From then on, his hostility toward me cooled down and he left me in peace, though still always on the lookout in case I made any mistake. There was no doubt that he wanted to catch me out, for I was the only Capo with the pink triangle, and a scandal to the camp, as he constantly put it.

I could tell of some other scandals, I said to myself, and thought of the tortures by his fellow SS men.

9

A "CURE" FOR HOMOSEXUALITY, AND AIR RAIDS

ON THE EXPRESS ORDERS of *SS Reichsführer* Heinrich Himmler—"Reichsheini" as he was known to both friend and foe—a prison brothel was established in Flossenbürg in summer 1943, known by the euphemism of the "special block." In what had formerly been the cinema, the hall was divided up into several apartments where the prostitutes were to live and "work." The special block was placed under the sick bay, so that a check could be kept on the health of the "ladies" and their clients. Naturally all this was the subject of great discussion among the prisoners, who had already heard about it well in advance. The "greens" and the Gypsies were most keen on the idea of a brothel, whereas the politicals were against it and held that it was simply a diversion on the part of the Nazis to conceal the bad state of the war. The Jehovah's Witnesses refused to visit the brothel on grounds of conscience.

Himmler's idea, however, was that those of us in the pink triangle category should be "cured" of our homosexual disposition by compulsory regular visits to the brothel. We were obliged to show up there once a week, in order to "learn" the joys of the other sex. Of course, this instruction only showed how little the SS leadership and their scientific advisers understood homosexuality, seeing a human emotional orientation as simply a disability and prescribing brothel visits as "treatment."

The same narrow-mindedness, of course, is still with us today, more than twenty-five years later, as far as most "authorities" are concerned.

One day the truck with the "girls" arrived at the camp gate and rolled up at the special block, impatiently anticipated by many people. Ten young women got out, and were taken into their quarters. They came from the women's camp at Ravensbrück, and were almost all Jews and Gypsies. The SS had brought them to Flossenbürg on the pretext that after six months of "service to clients" they would be released from concentration camp. The tortures and sufferings in the women's camps must have been just as bad as those inflicted on the male prisoners at Flossenbürg, otherwise it would be incomprehensible that girls such as these would have volunteered for brothel service. The promise of freedom was a gleaming one, an end to torture and brutality, as well as the pangs of hunger.

Believing in the promises of their concentration-camp jailers, they offered themselves up as victims for six months, whereupon they would allegedly be relieved by a further batch of "volunteers" from Ravensbrück. But rather than freedom, they were taken to the extermination camp at Auschwitz, completely exhausted by the almost two thousand "acts of love" that they had to submit to in these six months.

On the very first day, when the brothel was "opened," a hundred prisoners arrived at the special block at 5 p.m., four hours ahead of opening time. A similar number came day after day, with not the slightest letup. These prisoners, laughing and joking as they queued up outside the brothel, were by no means all men still in their prime—those were mostly Capos or foremen—but also included a good number of half-starved and exhausted human wrecks, floating between life and death, and looking as if they might collapse any minute. Yet they still wanted to have their "pleasure"—a clear sign of how sexuality is the most powerful of human drives.

"Dustbag" had holes drilled in the brothel rooms for himself and his SS underlings, so that they could get a good look at the "love life" of their prisoners and tell other prisoners the next day what position this man or that had taken. I often asked myself whether this inhibited sexuality of secret voyeurism through the keyhole was not more "degenerate" than my own homosexuality was said to be.[1] On three occasions I myself had to visit the brothel on "Dustbag's" express orders, which was already torment enough. What pleasure was I expected to get, when the poor girl lifted her legs and called, "Hurry up, then, hurry up!" so that she could be finished as soon as possible with a situation that was certainly just as painful for her? On top of which, I knew that some SS man would be spying on me through the hole. Certainly no "cure" was to be expected from this "enjoyment of the opposite sex." Quite the contrary: I was so shattered by this form of sexual intercourse that I never again tried to have sex with a woman, and my homosexual orientation was only reinforced.

Since the pressure on the brothel was so great, however, I was not ordered there again, though to keep up appearances I had to put my name down once a week and pay my two marks, sending another prisoner there to "enjoy himself" instead of me.

The camp "dignitaries" patronized the brothel very regularly, often bringing the "girls" presents, which might range from a

---

1   Amazingly enough, this behavior was not just mere voyeurism, but an express part of Himmler's plan for "curing" homosexuals. Any pink triangle prisoners deemed "cured" by virtue of their consistent good conduct in the brothel were then sent to the Dirlewanger penal division (see below).

sausage through to a pair of silk stockings. Naturally enough, the prostitutes looked forward to their arrival. Many of them always visited the same girls, and started talking in terms of a regular relationship. But this was a bit optimistic, for very often ten or fifteen prisoners would view the same girl as their future bride, and bring her presents. It was almost a miracle that it didn't come to murder between the prisoners involved.

Despite their regular brothel visits, however, the block seniors and Capos still maintained their dolly-boys, whom they were evidently attached to. I didn't blame them, for even though I never got intimate with any of them, these young Russians and Poles were both cleaner and more human than the worn-out brothel girls. But I suppose I obviously would see it like that.

Toward the end of 1943, a new instruction on the "eradication of sexual degenerates"—that is, homosexuals—came down from Himmler. He now stipulated that any homosexual who consented to castration, and whose conduct was good, would shortly be released from concentration camp. Many of the pink-triangle prisoners actually believed Himmler's promises, and consented to castration with a view to escaping their murderous persecutions. But in spite of good conduct—and this was assessed by their SS block leader and camp commander—when they were released from concentration camp this was only to be sent to the SS Dirlewanger penal division on the Russian front, to be butchered in the partisan war and die a hero's death for Hitler and Himmler.

On one occasion "Dustbag" asked me: "Tell me, you queer Capo, have you been castrated yet?"

"No, *Herr Lagerführer.*"

"Are you going to be, then?"

"Herr Lagerführer, I want to go home in the same state that I came in here."

"You and the whole pack of you queers, you're never going to go home again," he poisonously remarked.

What he meant by this was that we homosexuals, despite the promises of the commandant and the whole SS leadership, were not going to be released, even after good work in the munitions factories. The intention was to exterminate us, as had already been decided in 1938.

In any case, I steadfastly refused to be castrated, which gave "Dustbag" a new pretext to try and get rid of me, the only pink triangled Capo. "Dustbag" started a campaign for enrollment of German prisoners for the Russian front. The order had come from Himmler to fill up the ranks of the Dirlewanger penal division.

SS Standartenführer Dirlewanger was a former *Sturmbannführer* who had been court-martialed on several occasions, and initially imprisoned, but who had then been pardoned and given command of an SS penal regiment, just as the partisan resistance behind the German lines began to flare up at the start of the Russian campaign. His SS regiment, which rapidly expanded into a division, was made up exclusively of prisoners from the military and civilian jails, and deployed only against the Russian partisans.

Dirlewanger proved to be a dreaded and vicious bloodhound, a true jailbird to the end of his days. Merciless in his efforts against the partisans, he exterminated whole villages suspected of partisan activity. He burned the civilian population of these villages in their own homes or butchered them indiscriminately, even when they were only old men, women, and children. But he acted hardly any better to his own people. With the backing of the few SS volunteer officers in his division, he would also mow down his own men by machine gun in the battles against the partisans.

"Dustbag" thus drew up a list of "volunteers" for the Dirle-wanger division, with my name on it among the others, spite-fully saying that by serving at the front I might blot out the shame of my homosexuality. In this way he hoped to get the pink-triangled Capo out of "his" camp.

I immediately told the civilian staff in the aircraft factory of this "voluntary" enrollment for the Dirlewanger division, and asked them for their help. Since they were very unwill-ing for me to be moved, they telephoned their head office straightaway and told them I was quite indispensable at my job in the Flossenbürg aircraft components stores, so that my removal would virtually amount to sabotage of aircraft pro-duction. The head office was therefore to make sure that I was kept on as Capo. They also reported that I had displayed particular vigor ever since the start of my work in the stores, and had taken great pains to see that the supply and delivery of aircraft components went smoothly ahead. I kept a firm hand on the prisoners working under me, without any brutal-ity, and would keep them sticking to their work.

The head office got on Minister Albert Speer—so I later learned from the civilian staff—who in turn spoke with the SS department in charge of the concentration camps. The very next day the Flossenbürg commandant was informed by telephone from Himmler's office that prisoner X.Y.—that is, myself—was to be kept on as Capo in the stores of the Flos-senbürg aircraft factory.

That evening I was called into "Dustbag's" office, where the commandant personally informed me, in "Dustbag's" pres-ence, that I was to remain in the camp and continue at my post in charge of the station detachment. The commandant praised my careful and even "important" work in the factory, and took his leave in an almost kindly way, patting me on the shoulder.

From that time on, "Dustbag" finally left me in peace, and accepted me as a proper Capo, even speaking to me without any threats or humiliations, if he had occasion to deal with me, and never again so much as mentioning my homosexuality. But he generally avoided me, "Himmler's queer Capo," as he often referred to me to his SS underlings.

The camp "dignitaries" now also accepted me as a Capo equal to any other, despite my pink triangle, even the politicals no longer holding my office against me, though it was precisely the politicals who were the most vexatious opponents of their homosexual fellow prisoners. The majority of them are still so today, under our democracy, where many of them now hold positions of power.

Up till 1942, it was customary, in order to reduce the numbers of prisoners, for the various concentration camps each to dispatch a hundred or more prisoners at a time, at stipulated intervals, to the extermination camps, where they were gassed or killed by "injections." The list of those to be liquidated was left to the prisoners' office, headed by the camp senior, to draw up. If the camp senior was a political, you could be sure that, by far, the greater number of those prisoners marked down for extermination would be men with the pink triangle. After the war, I once read in a book how a former political camp senior arranged for the mass dispatch of homosexuals to the extermination camps. The prevailing feeling at that time was that the less valuable and less important prisoners should be the ones sent off.[2] That meant that we were indeed the lowest caste in the concentration camps, even persecuted and sent to our death by our fellow prisoners. This was in no way a "rational" feeling, for who gave them the right to set themselves up as judges over

2   This is very probably a reference to Eugen Kogon, *The Theory and Practice of Hell*, London, 1950, pp. 43–44.

us and classify us in this way, we who had done no harm to anyone?

In winter 1943–44 the air raids began. Although there had already been alarms at night, now the alarm had often to be given several times a day. When the siren was heard, all prisoners had to return to their barracks and remain there until the all-clear was sounded. There were no shelters for the prisoners, yet we were not scared by the attacks, trusting in the Allies' radio broadcasts that we heard on our secret receivers that they would not attack any of the concentration camps, and indeed this never happened.

The SS masters, however, had prisoners work day and night to build deep shelters for them in the hills at the edge of the camp, and scampered off there as soon as the alarm sounded. They could pose as heroes only against us defenseless prisoners; otherwise they were scared shitless. The SS guards on duty in the prison camp were not allowed to leave, but took cover in one or another of the prisoners' blocks, where they seemed to feel as safe as they did in their shelters. From this we deduced that they, too, listened to the enemy radio—despite the death penalty for this offense—and knew that nothing would happen to them.

When the sun was shining, we could easily recognize the Allied bombers, flying at a height of 10,000 meters or more. Hundreds of these silver birds glistened in the sunlight, flying wave on wave in formation. The air buzzed gruesomely with the noise of their engines, and our metal basins rattled against one another with the air pressure—a strange music.

We waited with bated breath to find out where the Allied forces would drop their bombs, for we, too, often had families or friends in the target zones. We could generally pinpoint the targets quite accurately by the force of the explosions, telling whether it was Würzburg, Weiden, or Bayreuth by the strength of the blast.

No matter how much we longed for the destruction of the Nazi regime, we could not remain undisturbed by the bombing raids, and none of us enjoyed them, out of fear for our nearest and dearest. The attacks would fall on towns where thousands of innocent people would lose their lives, people who had as much repulsion for the war as us concentration-camp victims. Perhaps the attacks were important to the Allies, particularly in their psychological effect, but they were certainly no cause for celebration. The bombing raids were accompanied by dive-bombing attacks, and we experienced these in Flossenbürg every week. They were not directed at the prison camp, but on the finished aircraft components that were already loaded on railway wagons. With unparalleled precision they knew when a train was going to move out of the aircraft factory, and would swoop down and destroy it with dive-bombing. Then the components of these prospective Messerschmitts would have to be brought back into the works for repair or reconstructed from scratch. Often these pieces came back three or four times before they could finally be delivered. We certainly had nothing against attacks of this kind, but actually welcomed them.

One July evening in 1944, everyone in the camp started running around, putting their heads together and whispering. I was quite surprised to be told on return from work that Hitler had fallen victim to assassination. My God, I thought to myself, let this not be just another wild rumor, but true! Let this butcher of Germany and Europe really have met his end at last! "Providence," however, intended otherwise. At midnight of July 20, the loudspeaker was switched on and we could hear our "beloved Führer" address us at full volume—once again Providence had saved him and preserved the German nation

. . . This damned "Providence," I thought to myself, it's just like the old Austrian emperor Franz Josef, who also survived through everything.

In the afternoon, already, the SS officers in charge had strengthened the guard on the watchtowers and gate, and in the evening, on return from work, all prisoners had immediately to go inside their blocks without any evening roll call being held. No one was allowed to go outside, which heightened still further the already blistering tension. After Hitler's midnight speech, permission to go outside was again given, but the watchtowers remained reinforced.

Subsequently the first transports of conspirators in the July 20 plot arrived in Flossenbürg. Officers in full uniform with decorations, soldiers, and many civilians. They came from all regions of the Reich, many still blood-stained from the blows of the Gestapo who had arrested and interrogated them.

And once again, men were hastily "injected" in the crematorium and pyres flamed to burn the dead, this time the victims of the unsuccessful conspiracy against Hitler of July 20, 1944.

"Dustbag" felt obliged, after an evening roll call, to deliver a speech in which he blamed the plot of July 20 against "our beloved Führer" on the "Jewish and homosexual International." Even his SS underlings laughed at this rubbish, as it was obvious to all that this was a plot by the general staff and officers of the German army. But "Dustbag" saw Jews and homosexuals hiding even behind the mutiny of the general staff.

For all his hatred of Jews and homosexuals, this time he really threw over the traces and ascribed us gays far too much influence in politics. This was the first time, moreover, that I learned of this alleged International of homosexuals. I only wished—and still do today—that there really was such an international association. But as I know only too well from my own experience, this is something there never will be.[3]

In the final months of 1944 the commandant gave orders that somewhat relieved the lot of us prisoners, and our treatment by the SS improved a little. Not that there were no more whippings or beatings on the "horse." But now such brutalities could go on only behind closed doors. To the public eye, the SS were somewhat less violent. This was the first sign that our Nazi overlords themselves no longer believed in a German victory.

Now soccer was played on the parade ground; that is, it had to be played, as "Dustbag" simply ordered that on Sunday block 10 would compete against block 11. The block seniors had to get some kind of team together, but this was not a team that wanted to play, or in which former soccer players could play, simply some eleven to thirteen men who were still physically capable of running around after a ball for ninety minutes, no matter whether they were keen on soccer or not.

At other times wrestling was staged in the bathhouse, in so-called block championships, with the "champion" receiving not a trophy but a loaf of bread, which, of course, was much preferable.

All pink-triangle prisoners, however, were excluded from these sporting contests. As "Dustbag" put it, the queers would just like to get their hands on the naked legs of the soccer players or the bodies of the wrestlers. It went without saying that Jews were also excluded from taking part. "Dustbag" saw it as incompatible with German law that Aryan prisoners

---

3   It's ironic that a man whose testimony makes such a contribution to our history seems to have had no knowledge, as late as 1970, of the first phase of the modern homosexual movement led by Magnus Hirschfeld, culminating in the World League for Sexual Reform of the 1920s. The very memory of this had been blotted out by fascism and reaction, and had to be rediscovered by the gay liberation movement of the 1970s.

could participate in a sporting contest together with "filthy Jews and queers."

The only purpose of these sporting activities, and the other minimal concessions we were granted, could be to distract the prisoners. To distract them from political discussions about the discontent of the German people with the Hitler regime, as well as the desperate situation that Germany now faced in the war, where the country had itself become a battleground.

But it was too late for such a maneuver to have any effect. All prisoners with any political interest knew exactly how things stood with Germany and the German people, and how the Nazi bosses were desperately still trying to dangle the mirage of a German victory. But Hitler's Third Reich was already at the threshold of collapse, in the very process of succumbing to the mighty blows of the Allied forces.

In Flossenbürg the "dignitaries" had other concerns than those of playing soccer or holding wrestling matches. We were worried that German planes might attack our camp one night, so as to eradicate from the eyes of posterity one of the greatest shames of the Nazi regime, and then blame this on the Allies. If this did not actually happen, we have not any humane stirring on the part of the Nazi leaders to thank for it, but simply the fact that they had no more gasoline left to fly with.

10

THE END, AND HOME AGAIN

ONE SUNDAY MORNING in January 1945, all German prisoners were called to assemble on the parade ground. Since this was so sudden and unexpected, we didn't properly know what the camp headquarters had in mind, and the wildest rumors flew round. With very mixed feelings we formed up in fives and waited for the commandant, who, so it gradually transpired, had an important communication for us. There were about a thousand of us, as German Jews, being "non-German," were not included.

After a good hour's wait, at about 9 a.m. the commandant and his adjutant arrived, together with the two camp commanders and a whole swarm of lesser dignitaries. All of them wore their dress uniforms, with full decoration, and made a great fuss about the occasion. After the camp senior had reported to the commandant, the latter began his address.

He emphasized how we German prisoners, by our eager and willing work in the aircraft factory, had shown we were still of German blood, and had performed valuable service to the Fatherland. We would also have the duty of defending this Fatherland, the Germany that belonged to us all, and which was now in mortal danger and threatened from all sides. The moment had now arrived when each of us could show that he was personally for the German Reich. He was able to inform us that from now on all German concentration-camp inmates were no longer prisoners, but would after a term of probation be accepted once more as equal members of the German community. All of us assembled here who were healthy and able would be trained in the use of weapons, and formed up in "werewolf" companies. We would be almost free men, though we could still not leave the camp. As an external badge, all "former" German prisoners who were able to defend their country and enrolled in the "werewolf" association would receive a white armband with the initials LP in black, standing for *Lagerpolizei* (= camp police).[1]

Now that he'd let the cat out of the bag, we marched back to our blocks with very mixed feelings. Many of us were against the military training, rightly fearing that we would be sent to the front just as the Hitler regime was collapsing, only to meet certain death. Other prisoners supported the idea, hoping to acquire weapons that they could use against the SS and the Nazis.

The "werewolf" companies, as the Nazis called their German partisan groups, were designed to carry out individual guerilla actions in the rear of the Allied forces, and harass the "enemy" militarily in the occupied zones of Germany. I shook my head at the very idea of training us concentration-camp prisoners as "werewolves," and said to myself: I am an opponent of Hitler's Germany, so its enemies are not mine. I had never felt myself a German, but always an Austrian. And now we concentration-camp prisoners, who for years had been beaten and tortured by the Nazis, humiliated and degraded, were supposed to help maintain their regime of oppression and racial lunacy, only to be put behind barbed

---

1 By 1945 there were about 20,000 prisoners in Flossenbürg, so the 1000 "German" prisoners (including Austrians and Sudetens, but excluding Jews and Gypsies) were a small minority. This explains why they could all be offered this "policing" role.

wire after performing our "duty to the Fatherland"—if we didn't perish first.

No, in no way; I was absolutely against it. The siren song of the commandant made no impression on me. As an individual, however, let alone a prisoner with the pink triangle, I didn't venture to express myself openly to the others. I simply said to a few of the Austrian prisoners—with whom I was later to travel home—"Look, Hitler's 'Ostmark' is at an end, and our Austria is going to rise again. It's up to the Nazi overlords and their supporters to play werewolf. We'll wait for the Americans or Russians to free us from the camp."

And so we did. We were indeed given the white armbands, which it didn't seem advisable to reject, but we were firmly resolved, if we really were sent behind the Allied lines to stir things up, to take the first opportunity we could to go over to the Russians or Americans and place ourselves under their protection.

Three German prisoners who took the promises of the commandant all too seriously and strayed a bit too far from the camp when they were out on a work detachment, feeling themselves "free" as the commandant had said, were shot and killed by the reinforced SS guard on the perimeter. From this anyone could conclude that nothing had really changed at all, and we were still under the lash of the SS. It was just that we were now earmarked as cannon fodder, designed to bring the Nazi overlords a few more days' survival and dominion.

The stoves in the SS offices burned constantly, as the officers sought to destroy all written records of their murderous acts. All files and cards on condemned prisoners were burned, along with the horsewhips and sticks used to beat the prisoners. They imagined they could obliterate in this way the shame of their rule.

It was March 1945, a suddenly warm day, when American tanks rolled up to our camp, surrounding it in a few moments and apparently bringing our imminent liberation. Every SS man in the camp, along with the guards on patrol outside, suddenly vanished and took refuge in the surrounding woods. The prison camp was quite unguarded.

The whole camp was filled with cries of joy. White sheets were hung from the windows, or spread out over the roofs of the blocks, as a sign of our peaceful surrender. There could be no talk of "werewolves" now, for freedom was at hand, and the end of our infamous imprisonment.

The brothel girls were fetched from their "special block" and joined in a rapturous dance on the parade ground, to indescribable shouts of joy from the prisoners. Those of us in the "camp police" had our hands full to prevent looting and destruction. The camp senior wanted to hand the camp over to the approaching Americans in good order, and so would not tolerate any excesses on the part of the prisoners. He let it be known, however, that in a very short time he intended to give every prisoner an ample ration of sausage, bread, and wine from the SS stores, which was answered by still greater jubilation.

Quite suddenly, however, the SS were back again and reoccupied the camp, and there was no trace to be seen or heard of the Americans. Everything had to be returned to its former place, and the prisoners returned to their blocks, deeply disappointed and downhearted, with heads hanging down. The SS vigorously took command once more, yet they were impressed that the camp police had not permitted any chaos. Life in the camp continued along its established lines, and everything remained as it had formerly been. Yet this was only surface appearance.

Even in the camp, now, there was an appreciable relaxation in the treatment of the prisoners by the SS, since even our guards could no longer believe in a German victory, and did not permit themselves any attacks on us. We still marched daily to our work in the aircraft factory, but no proper work took place anymore. We lounged around and discussed the approaching end of the Nazi empire, and how we could best return home.

A few SS NCOs had got hold of prisoners' clothing, planning to disguise themselves as prisoners as the Americans approached, and disappear in the confusion of impending liberation. Many of them, indeed, did do so, though only in rare cases did they manage to escape subsequent imprisonment and conviction by the occupying powers. Some of the scoundrels were so unashamed as to collect signatures from prisoners to say that they had always behaved correctly and decently, and never taken part in excesses. Some prisoners even signed, in exchange for a few cigarettes. The moment had come from our SS guards to reveal their true character. It was clear to me how they hoped to survive the collapse of Nazi rule and feared the rage and revenge of the concentration-camp victims they had oppressed so fearfully for so long. But had they a right to survive, after acting like beasts all these years? I didn't wish any of them to be killed, or suffer the same tortures that they had inflicted on us, but I certainly wanted to see them punished.

At 5 a.m. on April 20, 1945, the alarm was sounded and it was announced over the loudspeaker that all prisoners were immediately to assemble by blocks on the parade ground, together with their belongings. Every year on April 20, which was Hitler's birthday, a celebration was held, and always at that time in the morning, so as not to keep us from work. But we all realized that this was not the usual "Führer's birthday celebration," for the state of the war was too deadly serious.

In actual fact, the commandant informed us that the camp was to be evacuated, on account of the approach of the enemy, and we were to be transferred on foot to Dachau. He expressly stressed that anyone who could march no further, or who stepped out of line, would be immediately shot by the SS guards.

The situation must have been desperate, for we immediately marched off and the wretched journey began. The SS still had complete power over us, and gave us a final taste of their brutality, even though the collapse of the Reich could be felt in the very air. I had got together with five other Austrians, all with the pink triangle, and we marched together in this miserable caravan of prisoners. The six of us were resolved to take the very first opportunity to escape and make our way back to our own country.

The procession was to travel via Cham, Straubing, Mengkofen, Landshut, and Freising, but only on side roads, which almost doubled the journey. We couldn't help thinking that the purpose was not to transport us to Dachau, but rather to kill us off on the way, by exhaustion or by shooting us. Many prisoners collapsed during the march and just could not walk any farther. Even though the SS men must have themselves have been aware of the rapid collapse of their regime, and felt that the day when they would be called to account was fast approaching, this did not stop them butchering the exhausted prisoners. This I found even more contemptible than their previous tortures, for it showed how any human feeling was foreign to them, and how their fanatical support for the Nazi Reich would cease only with their own destruction.

Our way was marked by the bleeding corpses left in our wake. The local inhabitants were forced to bury our dead, so as to avoid infection, but they did so only very superficially, partly for lack of time, partly in fear of the approaching battlefront.

On the evening of April 22, we pitched camp in a recently planted wood in the vicinity of Cham. Quite exhausted from three days' march, many of the prisoners had feet absolutely covered with blisters. Already apathetic from tiredness and depression, there were many even now who would rather die than continue marching.

As we awoke in the early hours of the morning, however, a strange disturbance spread round, and we found that our SS guards had simply vanished in the night and left us alone. As soon as this became certain, there was no holding the prisoners back. The medical stores and kitchen were immediately looted, and everything reminiscent of the concentration camp was destroyed. A giant confusion reigned, and the years of oppression and enslavement by the SS were vented in a fury of destruction.

We six Austrians immediately got ready and slipped away, in great fear that the SS men might still be hidden in the vicinity and come and shoot all the prisoners down with machine guns in their chaotic celebration.

One thing we knew for certain: either the Americans or the Russians must be quite close, or else the SS would not have let their prisoners flee. We made our way cautiously and under cover in the direction of Passau, still fearing that we might fall into the hands of errant SS men or German military police, who would certainly have butchered us straightaway. At the same time, we kept a constant watch for American or Allied troops or tanks, yet still without seeing any. It seemed that we kept moving through the no-man's-land between the fronts, which was a very dangerous position to be in.

When it got dark, we stopped at a farm and spent the night in a barn full of hay. Now we were at last alone and in peace, free of the SS. The future was uncertain, sure enough, but could only be better for us than the years under the Nazis.

I wanted to go up to the farmhouse and ask for something to eat, also to inform the farmer that we were using his barn to sleep in, yet my friends were afraid he might betray us and hand us over to the military police. I put their minds at rest by pointing out that the Americans must surely be very close by now, and that the farmer would not dare hand us over to the Germans, as the Americans would surely destroy his farm if they got to learn of this. I proposed, therefore, to talk to the farmer, ask him for food and shelter, and make clear to him that it could only be to his advantage to get into the Americans' favor by treating us humanely.

The others agreed and we marched into the farmer's kitchen and spoke to him as planned. Our caution might seem childish, but we concentration-camp prisoners were so filled with mistrust for everyone that this was a natural feeling to preserve our lives. We didn't want to open a door that would bring us back into the arms of fascism; we wanted to survive.

The farmer, impressed that we had asked him for something that we might just have taken for ourselves, gave us a good meal. After we had eaten, he wanted us to sleep in his own house, but we gratefully refused on account of the desolate state of our clothing, and preferred the barn.

In the dim morning light we were woken by a loud rattle, and sprung up wide awake to see what kind of tank was approaching, German or American. When we saw the white star on the first tank, we immediately rolled out our white flag and ran toward it calling, "*KZ! KZ! KZ!*" The tanks stopped; they must already have recognized us as former concentration-camp inmates by our striped prisoners' clothing. The first tank opened its turret, its machine guns still pointing at us. We saw the head and shoulders of an American officer, looking inquiringly down.

As already arranged, I, being a former student, was to show my knowledge of English, and I said as best I could: "Sir, we are political concentration-camp prisoners from Austria, and request your protection and help."

The officer laughed aloud, and to the surprise of us all spoke in German with a strong Austrian accent: "Isn't one of you a Viennese?"

"Yes, sir, I am," I said, still in English, scarcely conscious that the American officer had addressed us in genuine Vienna dialect.

"Then speak German, you silly ass!" he exclaimed with a laugh, and jumped down from the tank to greet us.

The other Americans now came out of their tanks, too, and we shook hands overcome with joy. Only now were we free again, after we had yearned for freedom for so long; now no one would take this away again.

The Americans gave us piles of cigarettes and mountains of chocolate; they seemed set on feeding us to death. The American major told us how he had been born in the Leopoldstadt district of Vienna, and lived there until 1938, emigrating with his parents only eight days before Hitler's invasion of Austria. The second wave of their "wedge" would take us with them home to Austria, back to freedom.

We had to wait a few days in Passau, for the Americans were laying bridges across the Danube onto Austrian soil, and still expected pockets of the German "Alpine fortress" to resist. The six of us remained with the American tank unit, and were taken excellent care of at the orders of the Viennese-American major. In return, we helped in the kitchen and made ourselves useful, which brought us much gratitude and good wishes from the cook. But all the American soldiers treated us very well, and made a real fuss of us.

Finally we crossed back into Austria, and in only a few days reached Linz, with scarcely any resistance from the German Wehrmacht. This was the Americans' destination, for Lower Austria and Vienna were already occupied by the Russians. We were told that we could travel on to western or southern Austria, but should not venture into the Russian zone.

Since the Austrian post was again functioning, I immediately wrote home to my mother that I was alive and tolerably well, and would return home to Vienna as soon as I had the necessary documentation. After only four days I collected a letter from her at the post office whose address I had given. After rapturous words of joy, she advised me to go to my sister in Linz, who had been evacuated there from Vienna in 1943.

I greatly surprised my sister with my arrival. She was already married, and had a second child. Greeted with great joy, I stayed the next four weeks with her, and was cared for and looked after so that I could recover from my years in concentration camp. But it was only very slowly, with great delay, that my mental anguish began to heal. Time and again, especially at night, I believed myself still back in the camp. But my sister had such infinite patience and sympathy for me that I soon began to feel better; at last I had a home life again and lived in a proper family.

After four weeks' recuperation with my sister, I could not stay any longer, but wanted to return to Vienna and be with my mother again, having already learned from my sister of my father's tragic end. When I received the necessary papers, and was given an entry permit by the Russian headquarters, I traveled impatiently home.

My mother and I wept tears of joy when we met again after years of separation, with her ignorant of whether I was alive or dead, tears of joy mixed with bitter tears over the fate of my father. Yes, here we were again, she reunited with her son, now thin and drawn after long years of prison, and I with my ever-caring mother, who had never given up hope of embracing me once again safe and well, and had waited six years for this day.

I was back in my room once more, surrounded by all the books of my student days, a comforting and confident vision.

Everything in the very same place, quite unchanged from the day six years ago when I was called in by the Gestapo and never returned. Only we were changed, my mother and I: myself, by violence and oppression; my mother, by worry and grief.

I wanted to resume and complete the studies I had begun so many years before, but I lacked the strength or will for systematic learning. I could not banish from my mind the terrible tortures of the concentration camp, the dreadful and beastly brutalities of the SS monsters. I would be listening to a professor, but soon my attention would wander; I would think of the camp, see the tortures again in my mind, and forget the lecture. In hours of quiet, too, pictures of the camp would rise up before my eyes, pictures that I shall never forget as long as I live. Today, people have long stopped talking about the sufferings and killings of the Nazi concentration camps, and no longer want to be reminded of them, but we, the ex-prisoners, will always remember what we suffered.

My request for compensation for the years of concentration camp was rejected by our democratic authorities, for as a pink-triangled prisoner, a homosexual, I had been condemned for a criminal offense, even if I'd not harmed anyone. No restitution is granted to "criminal" concentration-camp victims. I therefore found employment in a commercial office, which hardly fulfilled my ambitions of a career, but nonetheless provided me with an income.

In the early days after my homecoming, the neighbors made a bit of a fuss about this "queer" concentration-camp returnee. But since I led a very quiet life and was never involved in any scandal, they let me go about my work in peace, though none of them went out of their way to be friendly. At first I didn't mind this at all, for I felt no need to talk to other people. Later, however, this rejection became burdensome and depressing. But whether we gays live in Vienna or anywhere else, we can live as decent a life as we want, but the contempt of our fellow humans, and social discrimination, is the same as it was thirty or fifty years ago. The progress of humanity has passed us by.

The death penalty for murder has been abolished on grounds of humanity, and this is certainly a good thing. But why are we homosexuals still treated so inhumanely, why are we still persecuted and imprisoned by the courts, just as in Hitler's time?[2] True, our modem "open" society accepts homosexuality in its own way, making plays and films about it, but at the same time homosexuals themselves are despised and persecuted. It is up to science and humanitarian organizations to enlighten people about homosexuality and put an end to this contradiction.

Until this is done, we shall still have to live in the shadows of society, and lead an existence that is not compatible with human dignity.

Scarcely a word has been written on the fact that along with the millions whom Hitler had butchered on grounds of "race," hundreds of thousands of people were sadistically tortured to death simply for having homosexual feelings. Scarcely anyone has publicized the fact that the madness of Hitler and his gang was not directed just against the Jews, but also against us homosexuals, in both cases leading to the "final solution" of seeking the total annihilation of these human beings.

May they never be forgotten,
these multitudes of dead,
our anonymous, immortal martyrs.

---

2 Homosexuality was finally legalized in Austria in 1971, shortly after this story was told, though as elsewhere, this is only the precondition for a real struggle for gay liberation.

AFTERWORD

From the Estate of Helmut Musatits

MANY PEOPLE HAVE SECRETS. Some of these secrets are revealed eventually. Others remain concealed until the end of the person's life—or longer. Close friends and family members live with these secrets and continue to harbor them.

Such is the story of Hanns Neumann. His secret was that he was homosexual.

Neumann kept silent about his homosexuality and concealed it his entire life. At the time, homosexuality was illegal in Austria and elsewhere. Women and men were punished severely for being homosexual, with jail time and fines—in addition to being excluded socially and professionally, rejected by friends and family. Homosexuality was considered to be "against nature."

These circumstances explain why Hanns Neumann did not want to publish the preceding book under his real name and felt it necessary to choose a pseudonym: Heinz Heger. Had Hanns Neumann published this book under his own name, he would have faced professional and personal consequences. Mr. Neumann feared losing his position in a large Austrian corporation—and with that his livelihood—as well as being ostracized socially. He even feared losing his residence.

Hanns Neumann resided in Strasshof in lower Austria. He lived in a small house with his companion and led a quiet life.

He was beloved and respected in his circle. Yet, in the eyes of his neighbors and some friends and colleagues, Neumann's companion was not his life partner but a foster son, a stepson, an adopted son.

We do not know what impelled Hanns Neumann to write this book. Perhaps he, who had the extreme good fortune to emerge from the horrific wartime unscathed, wanted to document the terrible fate of those who were not so fortunate.

Neumann was called up to serve his country in 1939. Toward the end of the war, he became involved with the underground resistance against the existing regime.

Neuman's estate includes, among other things, an uncorrected first draft of the manuscript as well as multiple versions prior to the printed text. In 1970, it was difficult to find a press that was prepared to publish such controversial content. Neumann received many rejections; some publishers had only superficial interest, and from others he received no response.

Since the end of the Hitler regime, countless men and women have fought to live freely, without repression, as homosexuals. Hanns Neumann is one of them. With his book about the persecution of homosexuals under the Hitler regime, Neumann has made a contribution to sexual self-determination—in spite of his declining to publicly acknowledge his homosexuality for the aforementioned reasons.

Mr. Johann Neumann died suddenly and unexpectedly on June 29, 1978, in Strasshof an der Nordbahn, in the company of his longtime companion, Helmut Musatits. Lamentably, Hanns Neumann never got to experience what an important work he left behind.

His life partner, Helmut Musatits, who took Neumann's secret with him to the grave, died on February 1, 2013, following a serious illness.

GLOSSARY

Anschluss	The German annexation of Austria in 1938.
Blockälteste (BA I)	Block senior, a prisoner with certain responsibilities for his block.
Capo	From the Italian (= chief), a prisoner with responsibility for a work detachment.
Central Security Department	*(Reichssicherheitshauptamt)*, combined national headquarters of all police and security forces, presided over by Himmler.
dignitaries	*(Prominenz)*, concentration-camp slang for the Capos and seniors.
faci	Prison slang for an orderly.
Gauleitung	Regional headquarters of the Nazi party.
Gestapo	*Geheime Staatspolizei* secret state police.
KZ	*Konzentrationslager*, concentration camp.
Lagerälteste (LA 1)	Camp senior, a prisoner with certain responsibilities for the entire body of prisoners in the camp.
Lagerführer	Camp commander, an officer directly in charge of the prison camp, but subordinate to the commandant of the entire concentration-camp complex.
Lagerkommandant	Camp commandant.
Lagerpolizei	The "camp police" to which the "German" prisoners were recruited in the last months of the war.
Obercapo	Head Capo, a prisoner in charge of a group of Capos.

Ostmark	The Nazi term for Austria (literally "Eastern marches") after the *Anschluss*.
SA	*Sturmabteilung* (= storm troops), the Nazis' mass paramilitary organization, particularly important before their seizure of power.
SS	*Schutzstaffel* (= defense detachment), the Nazi elite force that ran the concentration camps and also had a fighting role.
SS Hauptscharführer	Rank equivalent to British army sergeant major.
SS Hauptsturmführer	Rank equivalent to British army captain.
SS Oberscharführer	Rank equivalent to British army quarter master sergeant.
SS Obersturmführer	Rank equivalent to British army lieutenant.
SS Obersturmbann-führer	Rank equivalent to British army lieutenant colonel.
SS Reichsführer	Heinrich Himmler, national head of the entire SS and Central Security Department.
SS Standartenführer	Rank equivalent of British army colonel.
SS Untersturmführer	Rank equivalent to British army second lieutenant.
Waffen SS	The military wing of the SS, originally separate from the concentration-camp guards, but later amalgamated with them into a single combined force.
Wehrmacht	The regular German army.
175er	Homosexual, from Paragraph 175 of the criminal code.
IIs	Subdepartment of the Gestapo for "Control of Homosexuality and Abortion."

INDEX

Page numbers followed by n denote notes.

ABOUT HAYMARKET BOOKS

Haymarket Books is a radical, independent, nonprofit book publisher based in Chicago. Our mission is to publish books that contribute to struggles for social and economic justice. We strive to make our books a vibrant and organic part of social movements and the education and development of a critical, engaged, and internationalist Left.

We take inspiration and courage from our namesakes, the Haymarket Martyrs, who gave their lives fighting for a better world. Their 1886 struggle for the eight-hour day—which gave us May Day, the international workers' holiday—reminds workers around the world that ordinary people can organize and struggle for their own liberation. These struggles—against oppression, exploitation, environmental devastation, and war—continue today across the globe.

Since our founding in 2001, Haymarket has published more than nine hundred titles. Radically independent, we seek to drive a wedge into the risk-averse world of corporate book publishing. Our authors include Angela Y. Davis, Arundhati Roy, Keeanga-Yamahtta Taylor, Eve L. Ewing, Aja Monet, Mariame Kaba, Naomi Klein, Rebecca Solnit, Olúfẹ́mi O. Táíwò, Mohammed El-Kurd, José Olivarez, Noam Chomsky, Winona LaDuke, Robyn Maynard, Leanne Betasamosake Simpson, Howard Zinn, Mike Davis, Marc Lamont Hill, Dave Zirin, Astra Taylor, and Amy Goodman, among many other leading writers of our time. We are also the trade publishers of the acclaimed Historical Materialism Book Series.

Haymarket also manages a vibrant community organizing and event space in Chicago, Haymarket House, the popular Haymarket Books Live event series and podcast, and the annual Socialism Conference.

ALSO AVAILABLE FROM HAYMARKET BOOKS

Blood in the Face (revised new edition): White Nationalism from the Birth of a Nation to the Age of Trump
James Ridgeway

Diary of Bergen-Belsen: 1944–1945
Hanna Levy-Hass with Amira Hass

Fighting Fascism: How to Struggle and How to Win
Clara Zetkin, edited by John Riddell and Mike Taber

Loving in the War Years: Lo Que Nunca Pasó por Sus Labios
Cherríe Moraga

Marxists in Face of Fascism: Writings by Marxists on Fascism From the Inter-war Period
Edited by David Beetham

The Nazis, Capitalism and the Working Class
Donny Gluckstein

On Antisemitism: Solidarity and the Struggle for Justice
Jewish Voice for Peace, foreword by Judith Butler

There Are Trans People Here
H. Melt

Waiting in the Wings: Portrait of a Queer Motherhood
Cherríe Moraga, afterword by Rafael Angel Moraga

ABOUT THE AUTHORS

Heinz Heger was the pen name of Hanns Neumann, a writer who recorded the experiences of Josef Kohout, an Austrian survivor of the Holocaust who died in 1994.

Sarah Schulman is the author of more than twenty works of fiction, nonfiction, and theater, and the producer and screenwriter of several feature films. She is Distinguished Professor of Humanities at College of Staten Island and a fellow at the New York Institute of Humanities. Her most recent book is *Let the Record Show: A Political History of Act Up New York, 1987-1993*.

Klaus Müller is a historian and consultant for the United States Holocaust Memorial Museum in Washington, DC.